Not Forgotten

Not Forgotten

A CONSOLATION FOR THE LOSS
OF AN ANIMAL FRIEND

ALEXANDRA DAY

LAUGHING ELEPHANT   MMV

PATH to Progress™ is a not-for-profit program intended to
discover new approaches to the prevention of age-related diseases
and to bring new life-saving cancer treatments to pet dogs.
To learn more about the program, please visit their website at
www.gpmcf.org.

COPYRIGHT © 2004 BLUE LANTERN STUDIO

ISBN 1-883211-88-3

SECOND PRINTING ALL RIGHTS RESERVED
PRINTED IN CHINA

LAUGHING ELEPHANT BOOKS
3645 INTERLAKE AVENUE NORTH SEATTLE, WA 98103

*My dear
human friend* —

A door called death
has closed between us —
for the moment.

But could a little thing
like that break the bond
of love and understanding
between us, who have been so close?

Of course not.

Having left behind the body
which no longer served me,

*I can be with you
always and everywhere;*

on long delicious walks,

at quiet times,

and lively times,

alone,

among friends
new and old.

Let my excitement with life
still brighten your days.

*As long as there is a place
in your heart which is the shape
of me, I will be with you.*

One day you too will come
through the door, and we will be
together in glorious ways
we have yet to understand.

PICTURE CREDITS

PICTURE CREDITS

COLOPHON

DESIGNED AT BLUE LANTERN STUDIO
BY MIKE HARRISON

TYPESET IN PALACE SCRIPT & CENTAUR

The cover of my mother's recipe book

DEEPA'S SECRETS

Sunset over the Arabian Sea. Eight miles
from Thampy's father's house in Cochin.
Photograph by Shyamal Roy

DEEPA'S SECRETS

SLOW CARB | NEW INDIAN CUISINE

Foreword by Curt Ellis

DEEPA THOMAS

SKYHORSE PUBLISHING

For Thampy, Suneil, and Ahin

Contents

Foreword by Curt Ellis

"If we care about future generations fulfilling their potential, we must find a way to farm and eat that is good for the health of people up and down the food chain, and good for the health of the lands and waters that sustain us."

I knew Deepa Thomas was a miracle worker in the kitchen long before I tasted her remarkable cooking. Through my work as an advocate for rethinking the way we eat—first as a filmmaker of the documentary *King Corn* and now as a founder of the child nutrition nonprofit FoodCorps—I found myself speaking to a group of entrepreneurs and investors in Silicon Valley in the spring of 2014. I shared the message I've been trumpeting for fifteen years now: that if we care about future generations fulfilling their potential (and want them to have a planet on which to try), we must find a way to farm and eat that is good for the health of people up and down the food chain, and good for the health of the lands and waters that sustain us. After my talk, a man approached me with a warm smile. "I'm Thampy Thomas, and you must meet my wife. Deepa's cooking got me off insulin shots."

A few months later, I found myself in the San Francisco kitchen of Deepa Thomas. She opened a jar of fragrant spice and pulled from the oven a stunning plate of coconut-scented vegetables. With a painter's grace (Deepa is one), she made the art of cooking look effortless. With one eye on the latest dietary research from Stanford and UCSF, and with the other on the centuries-old wisdom of the Indian Ayurveda, Deepa remade Indian classics with equal reverence for good taste and good health. And with a life story as compelling as any I have encountered, from her childhood in India to her ascent as an entrepreneur and—now—her rebirth as a chef, Deepa filled our evening with stories that proved as exciting as her cuisine.

In this important new cookbook and engaging memoir, *Deepa's Secrets*, readers will find more than seventy recipes for healthy and delicious New Indian meals, and one master recipe for a long life well-lived: embrace every challenge the world sends you as if it were an opportunity; embrace every person the world sends you as if they were a teacher. Deepa's life is a testament to the power of such thinking, and her cooking is a testament to how much joy it will bring.

Beyond its filling and fulfilling contributions to our kitchen shelves, *Deepa's Secrets* represents an important addition to our national conversation about the way we farm and feed ourselves. With the scientific consensus now quite clear on the health risks inherent in the modern global diet—one rich in refined grains, processed meats, and added sugars—Deepa points the way toward a culinary approach that gives us all of the flavors we love, with little of the harm.

The latest think-tank estimates place the cost of our national epidemic of diet-related disease at $1.4 trillion per year. A little over $400 billion of that is the part we all think of first—the medical costs of treating a country with staggering rates of obesity, diabetes, and heart disease. But it's the other nearly-$1 trillion that

Thampy and Deepa

holds my interest most. That figure captures the lost economic productivity that comes from our workforce dying younger, progressing less in their careers, attaining less education, and achieving less than their potential in school. Follow each of those trillion dollars to ground, and you find a child growing up with a broken relationship to food. A child who won't have the chance to fulfill her dreams.

In my work at FoodCorps, which seeks to change the way children learn about food in school and to change the way we eat, I have seen first hand the urgency of reimagining our diets, at home and on the lunch-line. In one memorable example, a father in New Mexico loyally attended and videotaped our parent-child cooking classes, noting that "My wife already has diabetes, and my daughter is already pre-diabetic—we must learn how to cook in new ways for their sake." Indeed, we must create a future for food that nourishes our children's potential by first nourishing their bodies.

But as the memories and stories captured in *Deepa's Secrets* suggest, nourishing our bodies and nourishing our souls come hand in hand. Food is love, as the adage goes, but more accurately, food is about navigating our ties with one another and with the world around us. In Deepa's journey from the monsoons of New Delhi to the foggy hills of San Francisco, food became a source of connection and continuity to the culture and family she had left behind. Our relationships to

the people and places we have loved are not static— nor should the food be by which we remember them. The modern interpretations of Indian cuisine that we find in *Deepa's Secrets* reflect the principles of the Ayurveda and the passion of family recipes handed down through generations, but they also reflect the freshness, seasonality, and pace of our time.

Deepa's success developing a diet that freed her husband Thampy of his daily insulin shots should be inspiration for us all: it is a reminder that health is something we have a chance to control, and that food is, always has been, and always will be, central to our healing. But Deepa's story takes us further: to a world where amazing things are possible, and to a worldview where we are empowered to not just follow recipes for joy, love, and well-being, but to create them.

—Curt Ellis, *co-founder and CEO of FoodCorps*

"I'll take the risk."

—My husband, Thampy

1

Happy Accidents

സാംബിയയിലെ ഇന്ത്യൻ ഹൈക്കമ്മീഷണർ എ. എം. തോമസിന്റെ പുത്രൻ തമ്പിയും ഇന്ത്യാഗവർമെന്റ് സെക്രട്ടറി എൻ. റി. മാത്യുവിന്റെ പുത്രി ദീപയും തമ്മിലുള്ള വിവാഹം ശ്രീ തോമസിന്റെ സഹോദരീഭർത്താവു കൂടിയായ റവ. ഫാ. പി. കെ. ശ്ലീബാ യൂടെ കാർമ്മികത്വത്തിൽ എറണാകുളം സെന്റ് പീറോഴ്സ് പള്ളിയിൽവച്ചു നടന്നപ്പോൾ.

Deepa and Thampy's wedding ceremony, Cochin, Kerala, 1972, as published in the *Manorama* (local newspaper

Deepa and Thampy's wedding reception, New Delhi, 1972. In attendance left to right, standing: Mary Mathew, Thankam Thomas, N. T. Mathew. Sitting: Thampy, President V. V. Giri, Deepa, A. M. Thomas.

Happy Accidents

here is a commotion downstairs, and my sister comes flying into my room. "Deepa, long-distance call—for you!" This was New Delhi, 1971. A long-distance call was a major event. I hurry down to the kitchen and pick up the phone. Thampy Thomas is calling, all the way from Stanford, California, *America!*

....

"Deepa, will you marry me?"

"What?!" I said. "You don't even know me!" My sister must have stopped my mother from gasping into the phone. (The entire household was eavesdropping on the drawing room phone.) Thampy Thomas, with whom I had exactly *one* lunch date two weeks earlier when he was in town, after exactly one accidental meeting the afternoon prior (wherein he had never removed his hands from his hips, much less taken a step in my direction), was Minister of State A. M. Thomas's dashing, brilliant, eldest son—the state of Kerala's most eligible bachelor. I am twenty. I have a great job. My mother has been interested in marrying me off, but I wouldn't have said yes if Elvis Presley himself was on the other end of the line.

"I'll take the risk," Thampy says, with a big smile in his voice.

We exchanged letters for the next year and a half, and two Decembers later, Thampy and I were married during Stanford's winter break.

Saint Peter's, Thampy's hometown church, was filled to overflowing. And afterward, the seventeen priests, Catholic bishop, dignitaries, and villagers—more than two thousand guests (of whom I knew twenty)—sat down to a wedding feast: a late lunch, exquisitely composed on fresh banana leaves.

A week later, we were celebrated by another two thousand invited guests—among them the President and Vice President of India—this time in my hometown of New Delhi, at the India International Center. Long tables, cloaked in crisp, white cloths and dressed with polished silver, filled the lawns. High tea was served as the sun set. I remember my sari, beaded and threaded with gold, its glint, in an instant, a momentary grounding in the midst of a surreal experience.

Only days later, still caught up in the whirlwind, we were at Delhi's Palam airport. My parents were seeing us off to America. As I walked across the tarmac, I gave a backward glance. My mother was waving. My father was looking on with an expression I didn't fully comprehend until much later. He was steeling himself against the sadness. My father knew I was "quitting" India many years before I did.

It was a twenty-two-hour flight to San Francisco. (Roughly three hours less than the sum-total of Thampy's and my alone time up until that day.) We slept. And I remember waking up and watching Thampy sleep. *He's good-looking, but who the hell is he?* At 37,000 feet, it occurs to me. *I am about to create a life out of thin air.*

Fast-forward thirty-eight years to the day my husband gave up his insulin shots. An accident, not a calculated risk. For ten years, Thampy and his endocrinologist had managed his diabetes through careful titrations, two injections a day. On this night, five days into our new life—our new way of eating (which we refused to call a diet since diets made us feel "hangry" and deprived)—Thampy has simply forgotten to give himself his afternoon shot. He tests his blood sugar; it is normal.

"Let's just forget about your shot, Thamps—do it tomorrow," I say. And my husband, who for a full decade has been tethered to these shots, picks up the syringe and puts it away. He takes his blood sugar the next morning, and it is normal. We look at each other (the classic doubting Thomases) and wonder out loud, "Is the machine broken?" Thampy's blood sugar has been under control ever since.

We each lost over twenty pounds in the first six months of our "not-dieting"—eating three meals and two snacks each day, feeling satisfied and energized. And none of this would have come about if it weren't for another happy accident, a seemingly superfluous conversation.

I have made cooking Indian food simple and healthy for you, without sacrificing an ounce of flavor—just the rice and bread.

Three years earlier, I had convinced Thampy to move to San Francisco. I was ready to give up managing twenty acres in Woodside (something I liked to compare with painting the Golden Gate Bridge—you got to the end just in time to start again) to begin a new chapter in our lives. Our timing was perfect; we sold our Woodside place at the height of the market and scooped up a jewel box of a house on Nob Hill in the down market, just a few minutes from either of our son's places in San Francisco.

I had to give up my doctor, Michael Jacobs, and his wonderful wellness clinic in the move. It took me nearly two years to settle on a new doctor. I (knock on wood) am one of the 1 percent of women my age with no complaints, no chronic conditions, no "organ recitals," and no medications whatsoever. And I am equally proud of an unrelated fact: I am able to make conversation, meaningful conversation, with just about anyone. So, as my first appointment with my new doctor, Dr. Bobby Baron, is quickly coming to a close and all my attempts at conversation have fallen flat, I lob a softball. "Dr. Baron," (an associate dean at UCSF, my new internist is also a renowned obesity expert) "would you mind explaining the principles of weight loss to me?"

Thampy, 1972

He looks at me over the tops of his half-glasses (this is no *light* matter) and begins, "The first principle is to become very serious about exercise. The second, easy to say, but hard to do: you need to consume fewer calories than you burn. That usually means dieting." I'm hoping he'll tell me something I *don't* know. "Are you familiar with the glycemic index?" *Bingo!* "Agatston's *South Beach Diet* explains it—I recommend the book for its dietary suggestions, particularly to my patients with blood sugar concerns."

My homework for the six-month follow-up appointment! I buy a copy that same night. I read Agatston's book cover-to-cover over the next two days, and I experience my *aha* moment. There it is in black-and-white: rice and bread—two staples of Indian cuisine—top the glycemic index charts! *They* are the culprits for Thampy's high blood sugar. Moreover, they could lay claim to India's title as "Diabetes Capital of the World."

And then, I had my *what if* moment: *What if*, I thought, *I reinvent our favorite foods . . . without the carbs?*

Anyone who knows me knows that I don't have a dimmer switch. I'm either "on" or "off." I was "off" when I met Bobby Baron. My father had just died. I was done with my textile business, which had been my passion and livelihood for twenty-one years. I wasn't exactly searching—I have always believed that things find me—but Agatston's book flipped the switch. I threw myself head- and heart-long into this deconstruction and re-construction project. I studied the most successful diet books, the new crop of wellness blogs, a lot of ancient wisdom, and I had many long conversations with Bobby Baron (whom I now call my friend). The results were, *are*, life-changing.

The first two weeks of a slow carb lifestyle are no picnic. But, consider the first two weeks of getting in shape, starting a new job, or playing an instrument—you *will* survive them. And then you will discover that this way of eating is freeing, the opposite of what's known as so-called *dieting*. Thampy (keep in mind, the man is an engineer) no longer looks at his blood sugar numbers. The true test is whether he *feels* healthy. (We keep the machine around for backup.) I no longer obsess about my weight.

What if you're not watching your sugar intake? *What if* you've never watched your weight? I hate you. *Just kidding.*

This is not "Diva Deepa" cooking. You have not stumbled upon the tattered recipe trove of a natural-born chef. I cooked my very first meal on my second night in America, in the galley kitchen of Thampy's graduate student apartment. And when I cooked—correction, scorched—my new husband's dinner, I'll never forget the kindness of his grad student pal who quietly ran out and bought pizzas so I could put something edible on the table I'd set.

I quickly got to know Kentucky Fried Chicken and I worked very hard to improve. I had to; we were living on a grad student's budget those first few years. (Keema Spicy Beef, one of my old standbys, made it into this mix! See p. 186.)

Here's a little-contemplated fact: Indian cooking, the kind you've never been able to recreate in your kitchen, was developed in kitchens staffed by helpers. My grandmother's generation of women would gather in the kitchen on a Sunday. They had a hand in the preparations and some oversight, but the staff cooked and served the meal while *memsab* (short for *memsahib*, or *the woman of the house*) and her female guests shared stories.

My own mother, who was known for her baking (an English tradition), worked full-time and darted in and out of our kitchen. We never spent time there together. I went away to boarding school for my high school years. The best I can remember was watching our chef Krishnan putting the finishing touches on the plates before they made their way to the table.

I learned to cook in the United States, where I have enjoyed a rich variety of cuisines over the past forty years. As a result, my New Indian recipes are peppered with shortcuts, substitutions, additions—the benefits of my late culinary coming-of-age. If you are an experienced cook, you may recognize that I use *mirepoix*. Then again, if you are not, you may need a pronunciation key—"meer-pwah." (I did.) My New Indian version of the French vegetable mélange (p. 54) beautifully flavors a roast *and* cuts an hour or more off the traditional cooking time.

One more confession: I am a painter. (A disappointment in a family of scholars, but I'll save that for a different book.) I have taken a painterly approach to cooking. We'll begin with a little theory, and a supply list. Next,

I have separated out some basic techniques and recipes, like New Indian Gremolata, which stand on their own and then flavor later recipes in the book. Finally, there are the dishes themselves, the palette from which you will create meals and menus. I have given you plenty of paint-by-number options, but I invite you to go off-book, using the techniques and switching up the ingredients. Your kitchen is your canvas!

The recipes are intertwined with my stories, the kind I like to think were shared in my grandmother's kitchen. I invite you to take from my recipes and stories, all that you like, and leave the rest. (That's Kitchen Wisdom 101.)

Glycemic Index (GI)

The glycemic index is a rating determined by a food's ability to raise your blood sugar on a scale of 0 to 100.

High glycemic:	70 or more
Medium glycemic:	56–69
Low glycemic:	55 or less

The GI of pure glucose is 100. Low-GI foods release glucose slowly and steadily. People with diabetes can't produce sufficient quantities of insulin—which helps process blood glucose—which means they are likely to have an excess of blood glucose. The slow and steady release of glucose in low-glycemic foods is helpful in keeping blood glucose under control. Low-GI foods have benefits for weight control because they help control appetite and delay hunger.

Glycemic Load (GL)

The glycemic load measures the actual effect of a food on your blood sugar, which takes portion size (how much carbohydrate is in an individual serving) into account.

High glycemic load:	20 or more
Medium glycemic load:	11–19
Low glycemic load:	10 or less

To understand a food's complete effect on blood sugar, you need to know both how quickly the food makes glucose enter the blood stream (GI), and how much glucose it will deliver (GL). GI and GL are guidelines. However, as guidelines they are invaluable.

> *"Bus bus. That's enough."*
>
> —My big brother, Tomji

2

Right Foods, Right Mind

Tomji, Uncle N. T. George, and Deepa

Right Foods, Right Mind

ctober was my favorite month growing up in New Delhi. September's monsoons cooled the summer's scorching heat. There would be at least another month until winter's chill set in. And in October, we celebrated Diwali, which is actually short for Deepawali, the Festival of Light. Deepa, the name my father gave me, means light.

Tiny clay pots, the size of demitasse cups, holding oil and wicks, were lit, and they lined the ledges of every window on every building in New Delhi. There were fireworks and sparklers, and my big brother Tomji and I (all of ten and eight years old) were free to run up and down the streets. Small presents were exchanged among friends, and there were sweets. I would have traded all the rest for those Bengali sweets. *Rasgulla*, little clouds of heaven floating in syrup, with the slightest hint of rose and cardamom. *Sandesh*, dense, diamond-shaped milk sweets, topped with edible gossamer silver leaf.

"*Bus bus*, Deepa." *Enough*, Tomji would say as he popped one last syrupy ball into his mouth before settling into his homework at the end of the night.

Enough? I stopped, but I always wanted more. More sweets. More fireworks. More *Diwali*. More October.

To this day, I rebel the second I sense deprivation. Thampy and I were all through with dieting by the time I sat down with Dr. Baron. No more calorie-counting, puny portions, or crash plans. Although Dr. Baron and I never discussed it, my weight was up—it had been up and down my entire life—the classic yo-yo. And, I should admit that my so-called dimmer-less switch had been "off" for some time. It had been five years since I closed my business, Deepa Textiles. My sons were in college. My husband and I had made the move to the city, but that new chapter we were set to begin was yet to be written.

As Dr. Baron was getting ready to dismiss me from that first appointment—no noteworthy medical conditions, no noteworthy anything—I dropped the weight loss question, my conversational hanky. I was not looking for Dr. Baron's dieting tips. I was looking for *more*.

Deepa's mother, Mary, Tomji, cousin Joju, and Deepa

My mother reviewing Tomji's homework

*If only being "good" or "bad" were as uncomplicated as
what we put into our mouths. So, no dieting, no calorie
counting, no portion control, no deprivation, no guilt . . .
no cheating; just eating.*

Within forty-eight hours, I was in the grips of it, my *what if*: "What if I reinvent Indian food without the carbs?" *What self-respecting Indian would try?* Never mind that, my switch was "on." If I was going to do this—and by the looks of it, I was (I literally had all four burners going)—preservation of flavor (not self-respect) was my first and foremost concern. And, before we leave the subject, let's uncouple food and self-respect. Sure, eating healthily = respecting yourself. The problem with the motivation equation is that we often find ourselves on the flip side: we're "bad" on our diets.

As I embarked on my experiment, I returned to my roots in journalism. A critical reading of the bestselling diet books and most popular health and wellness blogs led me to the science of nutrition and the rapidly evolving understanding of the gut, before circling back to the ancient precepts of Ayurvedic practitioners. After five years of selectively keeping up with the field, I am not going to pretend to be an expert, nor do I want to add mine to the cacophony of "expert" voices already out there. I will simply summarize my findings, the uncontroverted underpinnings of my new un-fad food philosophy and the wellspring for all of my recipes.

First, carbohydrates. Simple vs. complex. Slow vs. fast. I'd rate the challenge of understanding them somewhere closer to complex. Our bodies metabolize simple carbohydrates faster than slow carbs. With simple carbs, we will feel hungry again faster, and if we don't eat, we will feel sluggish.

Slow carbs are broken down more slowly, which leaves us feeling full longer. This is where the glycemic index comes into play. As we know, the glycemic index measures a food's ability to raise blood sugar. Certain carbohydrates (including potatoes, pasta, and my former friends rice and bread) cause a radical spike.

A spike in our blood sugar levels triggers the pancreas to produce insulin and signals the body to store sugar as fat. Ideally, we want to maintain a constant, healthy blood sugar level by minimizing the spikes, which should also have us feeling hunger-free and energetic. The way to do this is by eating foods that are high in nutrients and/or fiber and lower on the glycemic index. And the secret is to eat small amounts of high fiber, low-GI foods like whole grains, nuts, berries, and leafy green vegetables *more* often, every two to three hours, which is the length of time it takes for your body to metabolize low-glycemic slow carb foods.

The hardest part of this experiment is letting go of the bad carbs—it is an addiction. I don't mean it's *like* an addiction; it's an actual addiction. Rats (say what you will about them) prefer sugar to cocaine. When humans' blood sugar levels rise after consuming high-glycemic carbohydrates, they experience a surge of feel-good hormones like dopamine. Their nucleus accumbens (the region of the brain that plays a central role in the reward circuit and involved in addiction) will light up fMRIs.

So, the first two weeks of a slow carb lifestyle can be tough. They were for us. You're going through withdrawal. By the end of two weeks, you will be feeling better. *Feeling better is also addictive,* the antidote to your carb addiction. You will become more attuned to your energy level and start to recognize your body's "satisfied signals."

Assuming you're already an Indian food fan, or perhaps aspire to more adventurous or healthy-eating, my recipes are full of the ingredients that are essential to your satisfaction. The high-glycemic carbs, it turns out, are not. What I've invented, or reinvented, is Indian low carb or slow carb cuisine. Not no carb, which emphasizes fat consumption. And let me throw another lens on it: it's not no carb in the sense that there is no zero-tolerance here. If you have a treat you can't live without, go on and have it! Just listen to your signals—have you had enough?

And perhaps the meatier question: is that treat what you were really craving? It took me fifty-five years to recognize my body's hungry and satisfied signals. I'm still wrestling with the cravings. Sometimes we just want something to chew on. Sometimes we have an appetite—something might taste delicious—but we're not truly *hungry*. And, if we're seeking emotional comfort or connection, foods seldom deliver (I'll come back to comfort "foods" in Chapter 12).

"*Bus bus*; enough, Deepa!" I hear Tomji lovingly teasing.

Have you had enough?
1. Your taste buds can tell you. When you're really hungry, those first bites taste amazing. Really savor them. Four bites or a quarter of the way through, the taste is less amazing. Your first signal.
2. Your stomach can tell you. Do a mental check. (Your belly is not behind your belly button—it's a bit higher.) You want to stop eating when you feel full, but not *too* full, say six on a scale of a stuffed-ten.

"Fortune favors the brave."
—Latin proverb, my uncle General Joseph's motto

3

Gut Knowledge

Maj. Gen. P. T. Joseph

Gut Knowledge

"When diet is wrong, medicine is of no use. When diet is correct, medicine is of no need."

—Ayurvedic Proverb

P.T. Joseph was a gentle general. A personal hero, he literally saved my life when I was nine years old. I had developed an incredibly painful condition, which we called lockjaw (tetanus), days after our family doctor had misdiagnosed my flu-like symptoms. Fearing for my life, my mother called her big brother at work. Uncle Joseph was the head of the Armed Forces Medical Corps at the time.

He excused himself from a high-level meeting and was on our doorstep within the hour, his staff car waiting in our driveway. I rode to the hospital with my aunt and uncle in that staff car with the general's flag flying (my parents trailing in our Hindustan 14, India's Morris Minor). He diagnosed toxemia (blood poisoning) en route, without any painful probing, instruments, or tests. I was in a coma for three days at the hospital while the tetanus retreated, and three days later I emerged to tell my tales . . .

Nearly twenty years later, I was visiting my parents, and a comment about what I thought was some sort of stress-induced stomach pain caused Uncle Joseph to palpate the left side of my stomach. "It's nothing," I told him. The MRIs had all been negative.

"Deepa, there is something there. You go back, and you have them look again, right here." The eye rolls I initially received when I quoted my uncle were retracted when a new round of pictures showed a polyp.

The advances of Western medicine have saved thousands, if not millions, of lives around the world. There's no doubt. But it's just now that the age-old wisdom of the East is catching on, rebranded as scientific breakthroughs in the West.

Ayurveda (*ayur* = life or lifespan, *veda* = knowledge) is Sanskrit for *science*. It is the world's oldest plant-based medicine, a healing science that originated in India over five thousand years ago. A "holistic" medicine (perhaps by the next century such an approach will no longer be considered "alternative")—the practice of Ayurveda is centered on the mind-body-spirit connection.

While I am proud to claim it as part of my heritage, I am a little embarrassed to say I was largely unschooled in Ayurveda until a few years ago. I knew it existed, but I hadn't looked any further into it. And as intuitive as Uncle Joseph was, Ayurveda wasn't something he practiced.

~~~~~~

"Let food be thy medicine, thy medicine shall be thy food."

—Hippocrates, the Father of Western Medicine

My friend Anila got smallpox when we were twelve. Her grandmother made her a paste, a "plaster" for her face, which she wore for a month, although it seemed like forever. Her skin looked like leather the whole time, and we teased her, like the good friends we were. Once that leather came off, the skin underneath was smooth. As beautiful as before. It never occurred to us to ask her grandmother to write that remedy down. It was buried with her.

More recently, my sister and I had a chance to visit my cousin Sujani, a cardiologist whose schedule keeps her hopping back and forth between India and the UK, when I was in Bangalore last fall. Sujani is a good five years younger than my baby sister. When the three of us were together, Sujani looked at me and said, "Deepa, your skin is so beautiful. Why do you bother with makeup?"

I guess I thanked her, and since a lie didn't present itself in the moment, I told her the truth. I had developed a touch of melasma, a series of dark or hyper-pigmented

My father's Hindustan Minor car

spots, since she'd last seen me. If anything, the drugs, peels, and laser treatments I'd tried had made things worse. So, I applied a little makeup to the dark spots and called it a day.

Sujani insisted on taking me to her doctor, an Ayurvedic doctor she'd known over the years to whom she entrusted her own medical care. A slight, unassuming man of very few words, he spent ten minutes or better just gazing at me, perhaps reading my aura. I was slightly uncomfortable, and when he finally spoke, he said, "This is going to be difficult to cure."

I looked at Sujani. She squeezed my arm and whispered, "He always says that." He gave me a mixture to put on my skin in the morning and the evening and an herbal pill to take. It's not a miracle cure—I am still on the treatment—but the dark spots have faded. I'm wearing less makeup.

The science of Ayurveda is sprawling. I won't attempt to school you in it here—no quiz on your *dosha* (mind-body type) at the end of the chapter. It's actually fascinating, complex reading, and there are others who have explained it very well. I will just include a couple of basic ideas, which I believe will resonate, no matter where you fall on the East-West spectrum.

On the preventive side, Ayurvedic medicine is really the science of the gut. *Agni*, or fire, describes a person's digestive and metabolic systems. A weak *agni* is something we have all experienced—feelings of indigestion. When food isn't digested properly, it sits in the gut. The nutrients our bodies need are not absorbed, and toxins, which Ayurvedic doctors call *ama*, are produced. A buildup of *ama* will clog the intestines and inflame the body's other systems (lymphatic, circulatory, skeletal, etc.) and organs, which can cause, again, things most of us have experienced—lethargy, fatigue, weight gain and more serious illnesses, like diabetes and heart disease.

I was thrilled to come across a recent medical roundup in the *Wall Street Journal* that explained it this way: *gut* describes a person's digestive and metabolic systems (esophagus, stomach, and intestines). The gut has its *own* nervous system, which scientists are calling *gut brain*.

To me, this is all very good, very old news. You may be predisposed to high blood pressure or heart disease. Obesity may run in my family, and my husband has a long history of diabetes in his. There are genetic factors beyond our control, but what we eat is an element of our health that we can control!

When I delved into Ayurveda, I was going back to my "roots." Not my journalism, this time, or my heritage. Obesity is listed as a "root cause" of diabetes. *Well*, I wondered, *what is the root cause of obesity?* Diet. Whether you want to credit Eastern or Western science—it's certainly not rocket science—we are what we eat.

And, it turns out that we are mostly microbes! Ninety percent of the cells in our body are nonhuman microbial cells. Our gut bacteria help digest our foods, boost our immunities, and help regulate our metabolism. With time, healthy gut bacteria, or microbiota, form colonies, which are now known to inhibit obesity, type 2 diabetes, heart disease, and autoimmune disease.

You can change the makeup of the bacteria in your intestines by changing what you eat *in as little as 24 hours*. Low glycemic foods are generally high in fiber and good for the gut—they give it a workout, cleansing and strengthening your digestive tract. My recipes are full of gut-healthy ingredients like beans, cabbage, blueberries, yogurt—okay, not all in the same dish. I have highlighted many of them as they appear in the recipes throughout the book. (With Western medicine's new interest in the gut, research has exploded. A lot of the current findings are still based on animal, not human studies. I looked for East-West alignment and note that results are promising, though in many cases they remain to be scientifically "proven.")

Dr. Mark Hyman, author of the *New York Times* bestseller *Blood Sugar Solutions*, observes that people on the Standard American Diet get Standard American Diseases—obesity, cardiovascular disease, diabetes, and cancer. Sadly (except for the pharmaceutical industry), most Americans then choose to treat their diseases with medication, not diet. I am not advocating going off medication without talking to your doctor *first*, but if she gives you the okay, or you can convince him, heck, yes!

One branch of Ayurvedic medicine emphasizes gaining higher consciousness through meditation. A lot of us don't have time to or simply can't sit and meditate (although we can sit with our devices or watch TV, go figure!). But I am not talking about sitting meditation. Now that you have awareness, begin with "mindful eating" by choosing the "right foods"—low-glycemic and gut-healthy.

Your day is full of choices. Your body is full of healing power. What if you gave it a fighting chance? Fortune may favor you, too.

Facts
100 million: Your small intestine has the same number of neurons as your spinal cord.

Your gut produces **90%** of your body's serotonin; your brain produces the other **10%.**

Gut brain reports to the brain-brain, and, interestingly enough, your brain receives more information from gut brain than it sends down. There is now a well-documented correlation between gastrointestinal conditions and psychiatric or brain conditions. Just as a nervous stomach can be caused by stress, anxiety or depression may be caused by a disruption to the bacteria in your stomach or small intestine.

> *"Come with me to my storeroom."*
>
> —My grandmother, *Mamma*

4

Kitchen Essentials

My grandmother, *Mamma*

Kitchen Essentials

he more I read—*South Beach, Atkins*, Skinny Girl, Fuhrman, Harry's Rules, Food Rules—the more I thought about my father's mother, *Mamma*. She was an organic farmer, locavore, and a model for self-sustainability some seventy years before it became fashionable.

When we were kids, the trip from New Delhi to Kerala, where *Mamma* lived, was three days by train—our annual summer vacation. The four of us shared a "coupe": my dad and I slept on the upper berths; my mother and my brother, Tomji, down below. A sleepy overhead fan moved the hot summer air from one side of the car to the other. We fanned ourselves, counting down the days, hours, then minutes until we got to *Mamma*'s.

Mamma's place was a kid's paradise. The country air was cooler, washed clean by Kerala's late summer monsoons. And it smelled of the wood smoke that came from her kitchen stove. Chickens ran around the backyard, and *Mamma* milked her cow right outside the kitchen door (and continued to do so well up into her eighties).

There were mangoes as far as my three-year-old eyes could see. My grandfather grafted and cultivated a hundred different varieties. *Mamma* would pulp the fruit and lay it out on long reed mats, where it could dry in the sun. She'd flavor it with lemon, and then, once it was good and dry, she'd add another layer of mango pulp. When her mango "bark" was an inch thick, *Mamma* would roll it up and store it in a giant ceramic barrel inside her storeroom.

That storeroom was paradise central, *Mamma* would let us in. She'd lift the lid of one of those ceramic barrels so Tomji and I could rip off hunks of incredible sweetness. The shelves, floor to ceiling, were lined with all manner of kitchenware, ceramic jars, and glass pickle jars, and the reed mats, which doubled as guest beds, were stored down low.

One afternoon, she let go of our hands to flip over a large overturned basket—it was magic! There sat a brood of fluffy yellow chicks on her red storeroom floor!

For your "Storeroom"

The notion of a storeroom is as practical as it is romantic. It allows you to plan ahead, or be spontaneous. Keeping everything you need just a few steps away is one of the first secrets to simplifying cooking and making healthy choices.

The following are ingredients that are called for in many of my recipes. Most of the items may be found in a well-stocked supermarket and the rest online; however, frequenting your local Indian market definitely adds to the adventure.

This is not a shopping list. Choose according to your preferences and budget. Buy organic, when you can.

FRESH
Broth, chicken and/or vegetable (p. 52): Or use premade, preferably organic
Curry leaves: *Kari Patta*, will keep for two weeks in the fridge and two months in the freezer. Freezer-spots are fine.
Eggs
Fruits: berries, lemons, limes, and mango. I love the Meyer lemon, a cross between an orange and a lemon.
Herbs:* cilantro, dill, mint, parsley, rosemary, tarragon, thyme
Garlic*
Ginger*
Jalapeño
Nuts: almonds (sliced, whole), pine nuts (raw), and walnuts (shelled halves and pieces). Raw is best, as micronutrients are lost in processing.
Onions*
Shallots
Tofu
Vegetables: asparagus, bell pepper, broccoli, cabbage, carrots, cauliflower, celery, eggplant, mushrooms, okra, (baby) spinach, etc.
Yogurt (Greek): plain, with live cultures

DRIED
Allspice (ground)
Anise (seeds)
Asafoetida (ground)
Bay leaves: Look for green colored ones
Beans/legumes: Chana dal (you can substitute garbanzo beans or split yellow peas, although they are not glycemic index equivalents; these substitutions have lower fiber contents/higher glycemic indices), urud dal, lentils
Black pepper (whole)
Cardamom (whole green and black)
Cayenne (flakes and ground)
Chaat Masala*
Chili powder
Cinnamon (sticks and ground)
Cloves (whole)
Coconut (unsweetened and shredded): You can also buy frozen, freshly grated coconut in Indian grocery stores or a dehydrated version online.
Coriander seeds
"**Curry" powder** (p. 26)
Cumin seeds
Deepa's Secret Spice (p. 24)
Fennel (seeds and ground): Lucknow variety, preferred
Fenugreek seeds
Fruits: dried cherries, cranberries, Medjool dates
Garam masala
Ginger (crystallized)
Ginger (ground)
Mustard seeds

Nutmeg (whole)
Onion (kalonji and nigella seeds)
Paprika powder
Salt: Maybe you are used to splurging when you shop for breads, cheeses, or desserts . . . splurge on salts instead! Himalayan tastes great, and it's loaded with minerals.
Sesame seeds (black and white)
Star anise
Tamarind paste: Tamicon brand is my favorite.
Thyme
Tomatoes (sundried and packed in olive oil)
Turmeric (ground)

OILS AND VINEGARS
Store away from light in a cool, dry place. Note: Fat is not the enemy. That's old school. Oil is beneficial to organs, especially the brain. Use extra virgin olive oil (EVOO) and unrefined coconut oil for cooking. Use EVOO (not more than 2 years from the harvest date) and infused oils to dress salads. From time to time, I will use butter instead of oil. Irish butter (made from grass-fed cows' milk) is micronutrient-rich.

Coconut oil (unrefined)
Grapeseed oil
Olive Oil (extra virgin)
Sesame oil: Toasted sesame oil is the most flavorful
Vinegars: balsamic, cider, red, white*

MISCELLANEA

Black beans (canned)

Brown sugar

Coconut milk (unsweetened, without additives)

Garbanzo/chickpeas (canned)

Honey (wild)

Liquid smoke (Lazy Kettle All-Natural Hickory)

Mango pulp (canned, Indian Alphonso mango variety)

Maple syrup (pure without added sugar)

Mustard (Dijon, such as Grey Poupon)

Oats (steel cut)

Pickle relish

Roasted red pepper (in glass jars)

Soy sauce

Tomatoes (canned): San Marzano, grown in volcanic soil, are my favorite—thinner skinned, less acidic, intensely flavored, and full of antioxidants.

Tomato (paste)

Worcestershire sauce (Lea & Perrins)

EQUIPMENT

Cast iron skillets: 8- and 10-inch

Green Earth nonstick pans: Affordable and PTFE- and PFOA-free

Rimmed baking trays

Wok

Tools: Immersion blender, food processor or blender, spice grinder, knives, vegetable peeler. You may want a mandoline to thinly slice your vegetables. (Mandolines and I don't get along. I rely on my lightweight and incredibly sharp Japanese knives. Bernal Cutlery on Mission Dolores, San Francisco is my go-to source.)

DEEPA'S SECRETS

Cheat and buy peeled garlic from the refrigerated section of your produce department. Store some whole, some crushed.

Ginger (If the skin isn't too tough, leave some on. More nutrients!)

For salads, sweet onions are less pungent than yellow. To further reduce pungency, slice in rings and rinse onion in cold water.

Chaat Masala: This incredible spice blend is Indian umami—powdered dried mango, savory spices, black salt. (Sham brand is my favorite.) Among a hundred other things, a sprinkle makes a simple green salad otherworldly. Just be careful not to oversalt when using it.

Buy cheaper balsamic and reduce by one-half on the stove for the syrupy, intense flavor of a more expensive bottle!

Wash and spin-dry fresh herbs. Then wrap in paper towels and store in a Ziploc bag for maximum life. Dried–fresh equivalent: You can substitute dried for fresh herbs and spices, using one-half the quantity called for.

If you don't see a fresh-before date, write your purchase date on the container. In general, the shelf life of seeds is one year. Three months (with peak freshness at 4 weeks) for ground or powdered herbs and spices, including those you toast and grind yourself.

If you plan to toast and grind, you won't need to stock the powders. Toast in a small skillet over medium heat for two to three minutes, just until fragrant. Careful not to burn. Cool and grind in your designated spice grinder. Store in a glass container in a cool, dark place.

Deepa's Secret Spice

Ingredients-wise, this mix is the wellspring (I'm going with source of creativity and wellness) of my cooking. I used to mail it off in jars to friends and family. After the first four dozen, I decided snack-size Ziploc bags would do. Fifteen-second gourmet: Throw this on a skinless boneless breast of chicken, sprinkle with lemon juice and salt. Roast it on a baking tray lined with parchment paper at 375°F for ten minutes, then lightly brush with unrefined coconut oil or butter (melted over low heat), dust with paprika, and broil until lightly charred, 2–3 minutes. Instant impressive meal!

YIELD: 8 OZ

Seeds and whole spices:
¼ cup whole coriander seeds
2 tablespoons cumin seeds
1 tablespoon (Lucknow) fennel seeds
1 teaspoon anise
1-inch cinnamon stick
10 cloves
1 tablespoon cardamom seeds
½ star anise seed
½ teaspoon fenugreek seeds
3 whole dried red chili peppers (whole dried cayenne)
1 teaspoon black peppercorns
1 teaspoon mace

Ground spices:
1 teaspoon paprika
1 tablespoon turmeric
1 teaspoon allspice
1 teaspoon black salt

1. Toast seeds and whole spices in a heavy skillet until fragrant and light brown (about three minutes), stirring constantly.

2. Remove from heat. Add the ground spices.

3. Cool and grind to fine powder. Store in a glass container in a cool, dark place.

It will keep for up to 4 weeks.

DEEPA'S SECRET
In a pinch, you could use a reduced mix of the following ingredients (add salt according to your taste).

Coriander *is high in iron and a powerful antioxidant.*

Quick mix for meat (yield 5 tsp):
Grind in a spice grinder:
2 teaspoons garam masala
1 teaspoon ground cardamom
4 cloves
½ teaspoon cumin seeds, toasted
½ teaspoon allspice
½ teaspoon cayenne powder

Quick mix for fish (yield 3 tsp):
Grind in a spice grinder:
½ teaspoon coriander seeds, toasted
½ teaspoon cumin seeds, toasted
½ teaspoon anise seeds, toasted
½ teaspoon fennel seeds, toasted
4 cloves
¼ teaspoon ground cardamom
¼ teaspoon ground cinnamon
¼ teaspoon ground fenugreek
¼ teaspoon cayenne powder

"Curry" Powder

There's no such thing as curry powder. I know, you can buy it here. However, in India, it is a cook's signature spice—the mix that brands a kitchen. This is mine—go ahead and use it in any recipe that calls for curry powder. Swear off the fake stuff. No more globby, turmeric yellow-brown curry. Promise.

YIELD: 4 OZ

Whole spices:
2 tablespoons coriander seeds
½ tablespoon cumin seeds
¼ teaspoon fennel seeds
¼ teaspoon anise seeds
¼ teaspoon fenugreek seeds
½ star anise
4 cloves
1 teaspoon cardamom seeds
1–2 whole dried red chilies
½ teaspoon black peppercorns

Ground spices:
2 tablespoons turmeric
½ teaspoon ground ginger
½ teaspoon cinnamon
½ teaspoon grated nutmeg
½ teaspoon asafoetida

1. Toast whole spices in a heavy bottomed skillet until fragrant, 2–3 minutes. Careful not to burn.

2. Remove from heat and add ground spices.

3. Cool and grind in a spice grinder. Store in a glass container in a cool, dark place for up to 4 weeks.

This is a salt-free recipe; feel free to season according to your taste.

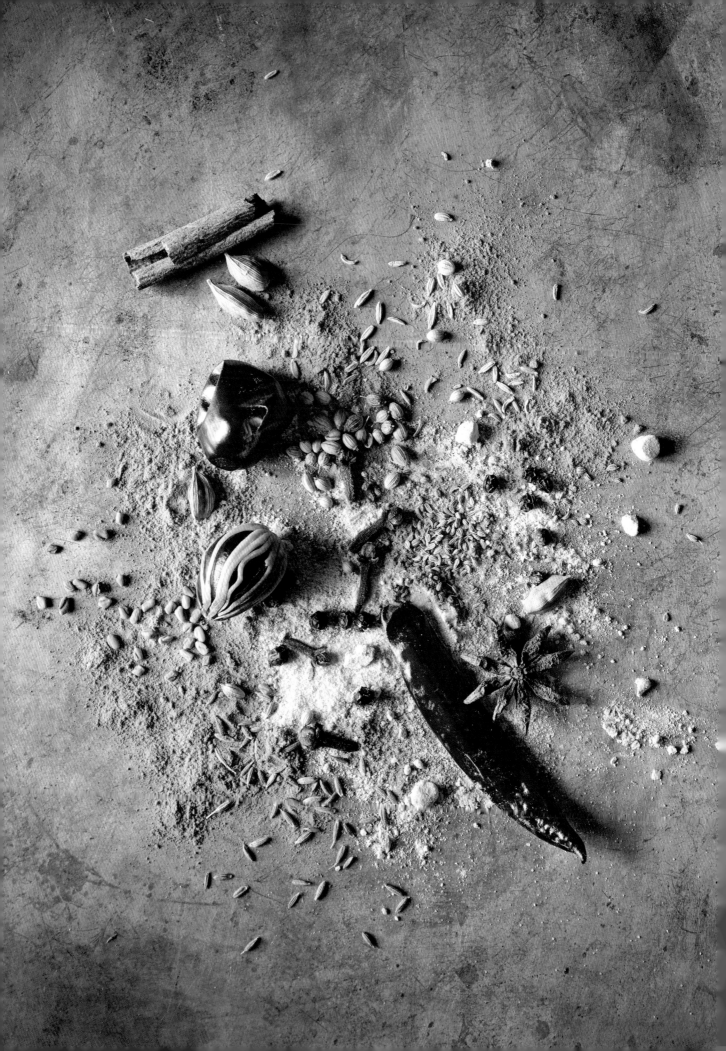

Magic Finishing Spice

This is my other secret spice—guaranteed to brighten every dish. Sprinkle on top of Caramelized Shallots (p. 58) and New Indian Gremolata (p. 60), or on dal, veggies, or grains for layers that burst with flavor, Deepa-style. You'll find Magic Finishing Spice used in some of the recipes in this book, like Heritage Barley (Better than Rice) Pilaf (p. 66) and Cauliflower and Beans Tumble (p. 138). Feel free to improvise. You could even toss with a salad and wait for the, "Mmm, what's in this?" I considered calling it "Jus'some spice."

YIELD: 1 OZ

1 teaspoon cumin seeds, toasted and ground
4 teaspoons chaat masala
1 teaspoon allspice
½ teaspoon cayenne powder
½ teaspoon salt

Mix ingredients and store in a glass jar for up to four weeks.

Allspice: Although it tastes like a mix of nutmeg, cinnamon, and clove, all-spice is not a mix. The reddish-brown berries look like peppercorns. They are rich in antioxidants and may help control blood pressure.

Deepa's Green Sauce

This is my new Indian pesto. A great dipping sauce, and an instant marinade for any meats, fish, or veggies you want to throw on the grill or into a roasting pan.

YIELD: 1½ CUPS

1 teaspoon cumin seeds, toasted and ground

1 bunch mint leaves, stemmed and rough chopped

1 bunch cilantro, stemmed and rough chopped

1–2 jalapeño peppers, rough chopped

½ onion, rough chopped

1 garlic clove, smashed

2 tablespoons fresh ginger, grated

4 tablespoons fresh lemon juice

1 tablespoon wild honey

2 teaspoons salt

½ cup water

Puree all ingredients in a blender. Thin, if needed, with more water to make a pourable consistency. Check seasoning. Store in an airtight glass jar for up to one week.

Mint: *Menthol, the oil in mint, soothes digestion. The aroma may also soothe anxiety and relieve chest congestion*

Mughlai Sauce

SERVES 4

Spice mix:
2 teaspoons cardamom seeds
15 cloves
2 teaspoons coriander seeds, toasted
1 teaspoon cumin seeds, toasted
¼ teaspoon cinnamon
½ teaspoon fennel seeds, toasted
¼ teaspoon ground fenugreek
¼ teaspoon asafoetida
1 teaspoon cayenne powder
1½ teaspoons paprika

Ingredients for sauce:
6 garlic cloves, chopped
2-inch piece ginger, chopped
1 teaspoon saffron threads
1 can (14 oz) coconut milk
    (unsweetened)
1 teaspoon salt
1 teaspoon pepper

½ cup grapeseed or walnut oil
6 bay leaves
2 medium onions, finely chopped
1 cup whole milk plain yogurt
½ cup water

2 tablespoons fresh lemon juice
1 cup cilantro, finely chopped

Drizzle this Mughlai sauce over *store-boughten* (as Suneil used to say) rotisserie chicken, and you have a gourmet meal. If you make the sauce ahead of time, and hit the express checkout with your chicken at the right time, this is your 90-second gourmet meal.

Make ahead: The sauce can be made ahead of time and stored for up to a week in the fridge.

1. Grind the spice mix in a spice grinder.

2. Mix the ground spices with the ingredients for sauce in a blender.

3. Heat oil in a heavy-bottomed deep saucepan, over medium-high heat. Add bay leaves and onions. Sauté until onions are golden brown, about 8–10 minutes. Add yogurt 3 tablespoons at a time, allowing the liquid to be absorbed before adding more. Add the blended sauce (from step 2) and stir for one minute. Stir in water (about ½ a cup) to thin to consistency for the Mughlai Sauce. Reduce heat and bring to a simmer for 2 minutes. Remove from heat. Check seasoning.

4. Add lemon juice to perk up the flavors, before serving.

5. For your winner, winner, chicken dinner: Carve and platter warmed store-bought rotisserie chicken, and drizzle with some of the Mughlai Sauce. Serve remaining sauce on the side. Garnish with cilantro.

Serve the chicken with a simple green salad with Zingy Citrusy Salad Dressing (p. 39), Kerala Quinoa (p. 68), and Quick Chana Masala (p. 134).

DEEPA'S SECRET
Carving tips? Marry a good carver! Or use sharp food shears to cut.

Cardamom: *The queen of spices has been coveted for its special medicinal and culinary properties since the beginning of civilization. Cardamom improves digestive, kidney, and respiratory functions, and the seeds are rich in minerals, vitamins, and antioxidants.*

Reemsie's Tamarind Sauce

This recipe is a shout-out to my forever baby sister, Dr. Anna (Reema) Tharyan. You have to get her a spoon quick, or she'll just drink this stuff.

YIELD: 1 CUP

6 Medjool dates (seeded and soaked)
1 cup tamarind paste

1 teaspoon cumin seeds, toasted and ground
1 teaspoon (Lucknow) fennel seeds, toasted and ground

1 tablespoon dark brown sugar
1 teaspoon cayenne powder
1 teaspoon asafoetida
1 teaspoon ground ginger
1 teaspoon salt
1 teaspoon chaat masala

Make ahead: Your Medjool dates need to be soaked in hot water for at least an hour. If you soak ahead, make sure to reserve the water.

1. Mix soaked dates with tamarind paste and dilute with reserved soaking water.

2. Add remaining ingredients.

3. Mix well and add more water to thin, if necessary. Check seasoning.

4. Store in an airtight glass jar for up to two weeks in the fridge, and up to one month in the freezer. Reemsie's Sauce is great for dipping and glazing—brush fish with olive oil and Reemsie's Tamarind Sauce before cooking.

Tamarind: Persian word tamar-i-hind meaning date of India. Tamarind pods grow on trees which can top one hundred feet. The antioxidant-rich pulp has long been used to treat type 2 diabetes in India.

Chutput Ketchup

Although it's not exactly the same stuff, Indian ketchup is just as popular as its American cousin. If you want to see Thampy turn ketchup-color, ask him about the time he used a whole bottle on the samosa his parents bought him from the street vendor. Your Chutput Ketchup is a condiment, a dipping sauce, and I use it to flavor a few of my recipes.

YIELD: 1½ CUPS

8 oz tomato paste
½ cup cider vinegar
1 shallot, finely chopped
2 garlic cloves
1 tablespoon maple syrup (or dark brown sugar)
1 teaspoon cayenne powder
¼ teaspoon ground ginger
½ teaspoon cumin seeds, toasted and ground
½ teaspoon chaat masala
¼ teaspoon fresh ground black pepper
½ teaspoon salt

1. Blend all ingredients well in a food processor or blender. Check seasoning.

2. Refrigerate in an airtight glass jar for up to 2 weeks.

Ginger Garlic Paste

You can buy ginger garlic paste, but, why would you? It's super easy to make fresh. Use a gob of this as a flavor base for any cooked veggie, meat, or grain dish. Store in an airtight glass jar in the fridge for up to one week.

YIELD: 2 OZ

15 garlic cloves, smashed
3-inch ginger, peeled and rough
    chopped

Grind to a paste in a food processor.

DEEPA'S SECRET

Very few things can be ruined, most things can be saved, except burnt garlic. Too much salt can be remedied with citrus. Too sour, with salt, or sweet caramelized onions. The only rule in my kitchen—throw out burnt garlic and start over.

Zingy Citrusy Salad Dressing

A little tart, a little sweet, a little spicy, a little heat . . . The flavor notes of this dressing bring back rainbow-colored memories of the sparkle and texture of my childhood in New Delhi. It's great on a salad, doubles as a dipping sauce (no double dipping allowed), and I also like to drizzle it on lightly sautéed or steamed seasonal vegetables at lunch time. Three uses, three times the raves at your table!

SERVES 4

4 tablespoons fresh lemon juice
1 tablespoon lemon zest
½ teaspoon Dijon mustard
4 tablespoons toasted sesame oil
1 jalapeño, seeded
1 teaspoon Ginger Garlic Paste (p. 38)
1 teaspoon wild honey
¼ teaspoon grated nutmeg
1 teaspoon chaat masala
½ teaspoon salt
½ teaspoon fresh ground pepper

1. Whisk all ingredients together in a glass bowl. Check seasoning. Use immediately or store in an airtight container in your fridge for up to 4 days.

2. Toss salad of your choice with the Zingy Citrusy Salad Dressing. Top salad with Go Nuts! (p. 44) before serving.

Nutmeg is the seed of the nutmeg tree. (Mace is made from its shell.) Ground nutmeg aids in digestion and is high in fiber. It also has a mild analgesic compound and has long been used as a home remedy for insomnia and as an antidepressant.

DEEPA'S SECRET
Honey, read carefully! Check the ingredients. Many brands are flavored with sugar (bad!). Same goes for maple syrup.

Quick Onion Pickle

Moti Mahal was a special treat restaurant in the Delhi of my childhood. It is still open for business in Delhi, but not quite as *dhaba*-ish (hole-in-the-wall)! All the tandoori dishes were drool-worthy, but it was that "free" condiment that was on every table—pickled onion, oh my! This adaptation is an homage to a delicious memory.

YIELD: 4 OZ

Pickling liquid:
1 cup white vinegar
1 cup water
¼ teaspoon cayenne powder
6 curry leaves
½ teaspoon brown sugar
1 teaspoon salt

1 red onion, sliced into ¼-inch rings

1. Bring pickling liquid ingredients to a boil in a small deep saucepan.

2. Add onion slices and cover. Turn heat off and keep covered for 15 minutes.

3. Cool and store in a jar. Keeps for up to 2 weeks in the fridge.

Sucy Mathews

YIELD: 8 CUPS

Lemons:
10 lemons
2 tablespoons grapeseed oil
2 tablespoons salt
4 teaspoons sugar

Caramelized sugar:
3 tablespoons sugar
2 tablespoons water

Date and raisin paste:
⅔ cup Medjool dates (pitted)
5 tablespoons white vinegar, divided
½ cup golden raisins

Pickle base:
1 cup grapeseed oil
1 tablespoon mustard seeds
4 tablespoons Ginger Garlic Paste (p. 38)
2 teaspoons cumin seeds, toasted and
   ground
10 curry leaves
2 teaspoons cayenne powder
¼ teaspoon asafoetida
¼ teaspoon ground fenugreek
1 tablespoon paprika
1 tablespoon salt
1 cup white vinegar

Vinegar: *Claims that vinegar lowers blood sugar levels have been made since Hippocrates's time. Scientists are currently researching its antiglycemic effect.*

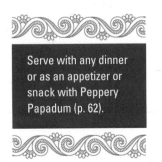

Serve with any dinner or as an appetizer or snack with Peppery Papadum (p. 62).

Sucy's Lemon Pickle with Medjool Dates

My amazing sister-in-law Sucy Mathews is a brave cancer survivor and a fabulous cook. Just last year, Thampy and I went to visit and take care of her—she ended up taking care of us. And, we learned to make her signature lemon pickle. You'll see why this pickle gets rave reviews!

Make ahead: The lemons need to dry out for 3–4 days before seasoning. The pickle base can be made earlier and stored in a lidded jar at room temperature while the lemons are drying.

1. Steam lemons in a colander (or steamer) over hot water in a deep saucepan (covered) for 3 minutes. Remove and wipe dry.

2. In a cast-iron pan, heat grapeseed oil. Fry lemons, several at a time (don't crowd the pan), until they begin to brown all over. (Don't worry if some juice escapes.) Continue until all the lemons are browned. Wipe lemons with paper towels to remove any blackened lemon skin. This will keep the skin from tasting bitter.

3. Cut lemons into four wedges over a bowl, reserving juice. Add salt and sugar to the lemon pieces (and juice), and transfer to your pickle jar. Place the lidded jar in the sun for 3–4 days (a sunny windowsill will work fine).

4. For the caramelized sugar: Heat 3 tablespoons of sugar in a small saucepan until it is the color of maple syrup. (Do not stir.) Add 2 tablespoons of water. Be careful, shield yourself with a lid, the stuff spits! Remove from heat and stir.

5. For the date and raisin paste: Grind half of the Medjool dates with 3 tablespoons of vinegar in a food processor to make a paste. Chop the other half. Grind half the golden raisins with 2 tablespoons of vinegar to make a paste. Mix the date and raisin pastes with the chopped dates and remaining (whole) raisins.

6. For the pickle base: In a deep, 12-inch saucepan, heat grapeseed oil until it starts to shimmer. Drop a couple of mustard seeds in—the oil is ready when the seeds "pop." Add the mustard seeds, shielding yourself with a lid. Add Ginger Garlic Paste, then cumin seeds, curry leaves, and the remaining spices (including the last tablespoon of salt). Add date and raisin mixture, and stir for one minute. Then, add caramelized sugar and one cup of white vinegar. Lower heat and simmer for 5 minutes.

7. Add sun-dried lemons with their juice to the pickle base and simmer for 5 minutes. Cool and store in a mason jar. Refrigerate for a longer shelf life.

Go Nuts!

Get out your biggest jar, then go buy one that's twice that big. I am always reaching for this micronutrient-rich mix—a handful over yogurt and berries. Another at snack time. Again, on top of a salad . . . It's nuts!

YIELD: 7 CUPS

Seeds and nuts:
1 cup walnuts
1 cup pine nuts
1 cup sliced almonds
2 cups sunflower seeds
2 cups pumpkin seeds

¼ teaspoon cayenne powder
1 teaspoon salt (truffle salt if you like)

1. Toast the seeds and nuts in a pan over medium heat until light brown (about 4 minutes), stirring constantly.

2. Remove from heat and sprinkle with cayenne powder and salt. Store in an airtight glass jar for up to two weeks.

Walnuts: *They're good for your heart and chock-full of healthy fats and omega-3 fatty acids. Several studies also suggest they may reduce the risk of type 2 diabetes.*

Deepa, 5 years old

Spicy Snacking Peanuts

I'm constantly running out of these peanuts. They are great for snacking, or, when rough-chopped, as a topping—an extra layer of crunchy, spicy goodness on top of salads, veggies, meat—just about everything!

YIELD: 3 CUPS

1 teaspoon unrefined coconut oil
8 curry leaves
3 cups Indian or Spanish peanuts
    (small, with skin)
¼ teaspoon cumin seeds, toasted
    and ground
¼ teaspoon cayenne powder
¼ teaspoon garam masala
½ teaspoon chaat masala

½ teaspoon salt

1. Heat oil in a 10-inch cast-iron skillet over medium heat. Add curry leaves and peanuts, taking care to shield yourself with a lid as curry leaves will splutter. Stir peanuts until they begin to brown, about 2 minutes.

2. Remove from heat and stir in remaining ingredients, except salt. Check seasoning (chaat masala has black salt in it) before adding salt.

3. Cool and store in a glass jar for up to 2 weeks. Warm before serving.

Peanut: *Not a nut, but closer to a pea, the peanut is a legume—same family as the pea and bean. It is full of monounsaturated (good) fat, other heart-healthy nutrients, and antioxidants.*

"When you are aware, you can make choices—not about your perceptions, but about how you assign meaning to them."

—Professor Luthra, Delhi University

5

The Basics

The Basics

There's a flavor burst or boost associated with each layer—a la Willy Wonka's Gobstopper—all delivered in one forkful.

"Y ou see four legs, you are convinced it is a table." Professor Luthra rapped the table under her lectern. "What about a chair?" She sat on it. "A desk, of course. A bed? A shelter. This," she said, rapping again, "can be anything you want it to be."

We were sitting in a "Political Thought" class, not "The Philosophy of Perceptual Experience." Professor Luthra, bless her, was attempting to pry open our minds and plant a tiny seed of awareness. "When you are aware, you can make choices—not about your perceptions, but about how you assign meaning to them."

That seed stayed buried for about thirty-five years when it came to my outlook on food, which (as a clue to my general obliviousness) could have been previously pinpointed midrange on the *eat to live–live to eat* spectrum, with my weight swinging twenty-five pounds in either direction. When I set my mind to recreating our favorite recipes without carbs, I began with Thampy's family dishes. Doctoring wasn't even an option as none of these recipes had been committed to writing. I literally started with the end results. "This is a curry." *What is a curry?* After a few weeks of experimentation, I had the answer. A curry, essentially,

is a *flavor*, which infuses foods through cooking. The foods themselves were surprisingly unimportant. It was all in the flavor and the cooking, a process that would concentrate the flavor and maintain the mouthfeel of the dish. Cook time is critical—I'm not talking about the endless hours my foremothers spent over steaming pots—just minutes. Under- or over-cooking can make a big difference.

Necessity became the mother of this reinvention. Or, as I used to say when the boys were small, mothering makes reinvention necessary. Few of us have time for labor-intensive food preparation. I have developed a unique process, the combined "gift" of my total lack of experience in the kitchen with the true gift of shared experiences in the kitchens of the masterful chefs I've been lucky enough to call friends. I liken it to a painterly approach—working with palette of materials (since I'm a painter). A friend suggested it is rather

"*Tadka*"

(pronounced "thud-ka") This is simply oil infused with seeds and spices, then used as a base to caramelize onions or shallots, all of which become a topping.

architectural: building on a foundation. It's a process of layering, and you have my full permission to apply your own professional metaphor.

Here's how it works (this is just an overview, the recipes will walk you through all the steps):

A flavor "base" (a mix of seeds, spices, chopped onion, ginger/garlic paste, etc. that can be made ahead of time and stored) is used to infuse hot oil. Then your "mains" (meat/fish and/or vegetables) are added. These are "topped" with another layer of flavor (Caramelized Shallots [p. 58] or a New Indian Gremolata [p. 60], which, again, can be premade and kept in the fridge at the ready), or nuts and finished with a "dusting" of spice or zest.

Tadka (pronounced "thud-ka"): A little new vocabulary to go with your new recipes . . . You'll notice a *tadka* layer in several of my dishes. This is simply oil infused with seeds and spices, then used as a base to caramelize onions or shallots, all of which become a topping. It's the fusion process—some reverse-engineering that gives me creamy mushroom soup, for example, without a spot of cream. But it's not the flavor muddle of some of what passes for fusion cuisine. There's a flavor burst or boost associated with each layer—a la Willy Wonka's Gobstopper—all delivered in one forkful.

Wait, where's the rice? Did I hear you asking? With my new food outlook, I ask myself two questions: *Is it delicious?* and *Is it good for me?* In this case, does rice *add* flavor? Plain rice—*no*. If I fancied it up—sure, but that's more work; and will it then enhance the other layers? Debatable. And I don't have to take sides because I already know the answer to my second question: Is it good for me? No.

We "eat" with our eyes first.

Rice is all about mouthfeel. It's comfort food, I'll give you that. Could I interest you in a side of barley pilaf instead? Or, dare you to try it without?

Once you get the hang of layering, you can go off-book, off-continent—same technique, different flavors, mains, toppings, dustings. And before you try your layering, I mean, before you take that first forkful, pause to look at your plate. There's another layer to perceptual experience: We "eat" with our eyes first. I can almost see Professor Luthra winking at me.

Sosamma's Basic Broth

Sosamma to her childhood friends and family (or Mary Mathew when she headed up the YWCA and received the Queen of England in 1961), my mom was a sensational cook. Her soups gave a warm welcome to guests on a chilly New Delhi winter evening. This basic broth could pass for an elegant soup, ladled, steaming, into fine china teacups, and garnished with croutons that gently capsized into the deliciousness on the way to the table!

YIELD: 4 QUARTS

Sauté ingredients:
2 tablespoons extra virgin olive oil
4 onions, sliced
1 bay leaf
2 cardamom pods
1 stick cinnamon
2 cloves

Dried spices:
1 teaspoon cumin seeds, toasted
   and ground
1 teaspoon fennel seeds, toasted
   and ground
1 teaspoon dried thyme
1 tablespoon black peppercorns
1 tablespoon salt

Vegetables:
4 cups (½ lb) baby spinach
2 cups mushrooms, sliced
1 onion, sliced
2 zucchini, cubed
1 green bell pepper, rough chopped
3 celery stalks, cut into 2-inch pieces
1 carrot, cut into 2-inch pieces
1 fennel bulb, rough chopped
4 garlic cloves, whole, smashed with the
   back of a flat knife
1 potato, rough chopped, unpeeled is
   fine
2 tomatoes, quartered
1 bunch parsley, rough chopped

1 whole chicken, patted dry
3 quarts water

Optional (for extra fiber):
1 cup chana dal, well-rinsed and drained

This recipe works for a vegetarian version if you leave the chicken out.

1. Heat oil in a soup pot over medium heat. Add sauté ingredients. Sauté for 3 minutes. Lower temperature, cover, and cook for 10 minutes, stirring occasionally until onions begin to brown and soften.

2. Add remaining ingredients, including the dried spices, vegetables, chicken (if using), and water. Chana dal can be added at this stage. Cover and simmer for one hour.

3. Cool slightly and strain through a colander, pressing down on all of the ingredients before discarding. Check seasoning.

DEEPA'S SECRET

A Sosamma chicken broth ritual: Bone the chicken, and throw the meat back in, along with some whole grain pasta, sliced cabbage, a little salt, and fresh black pepper. Irresistible soup!

Gelatin: Bone broth is a staple of gut-healthy diets. A well-known anti-inflammatory, the gelatin in bone also restores the mucosal lining of the stomach and promotes the secretion of gastric acid aiding in the digestion of nutrients. Sosamma's chicken soup has proven curative powers!

New Indian Mirepoix

Every culture has a way of flavoring the oil as a base to a dish with a vegetable and herb combination. The French have mirepoix. My New Indian Mirepoix provides a flavor platform for anything from a soup or stew to a roast. Use it as a base for your next creation when you make your favorite soup or entree. Easy peasy delicious!

YIELD: 2 CUPS

Seeds for infused oil:
2 tablespoons unrefined coconut oil
½ teaspoon black mustard seeds
½ teaspoon cumin seeds
½ teaspoon (Lucknow) fennel seeds

Whole spices for infused oil:
2 cloves
1 cardamom pod
2-inch cinnamon stick
6 curry leaves

Flavor base:
2 cups onion, finely chopped
1–2 jalapeños, slit and seeded
6 garlic cloves, minced
½-inch piece fresh ginger, grated
1 bay leaf

Aroma ingredients:
1 teaspoon turmeric
2 teaspoons Deepa's Secret Spice (p. 24)
½ teaspoon fresh ground black pepper
1 teaspoon salt

½ cup water

1. Heat oil in a heavy saucepan over medium heat. When shimmering, add seeds. Add whole spices and stir for 30 seconds. Shield yourself with a lid as the seeds pop and curry leaves splutter in the hot oil.

2. Add onion and brown until golden (about 5 minutes). Add the remaining flavor base ingredients, and sauté for 3 minutes.

3. Add aroma ingredients, reduce heat and stir for 1 minute. Add ½ cup of water. Stir until the water evaporates and the base thickens.

4. Now it's up to you. Make this New Indian Mirepoix the base for your inventions. Just add about 2 lbs of meat, seafood, or veggies. Cook like you would a full-flavored stew. Going off-book is always fun. Top the entrée you just made with New Indian Gremolata (p. 60). I like to leave the cinnamon stick as a garnish in the finished dish. It looks pretty!

Double or triple the recipe, then divide and freeze in airtight glass containers for future meals. New Indian Mirepoix will keep for up to one week in your fridge, and one month in the freezer.

Dal for Dummies!

My uncle, General Joseph, had dal at lunch. Nair, his chef, made it every day, and it always surprised me how something so ordinary tasted anything but. I've recreated Nair's dal here.

SERVES 4

1 cup chana dal, soaked overnight
½ teaspoon turmeric
1 teaspoon salt
1 teaspoon fresh ground black pepper

Tadka:
2 tablespoons grapeseed (or your
   favorite) oil
1 teaspoon black mustard seeds
1 teaspoon (Lucknow) fennel seeds
1 teaspoon cumin seeds
½ red onion, sliced
1 jalapeño, cut from top to tip 4 times,
   leaving top in place (remove seeds
   for less heat)
2 garlic cloves, thinly sliced
½ teaspoon cayenne flakes
1 tomato, sliced

1 tablespoon fresh ginger, grated

Crowning flavor:
1 tablespoon butter
1 cup cilantro, stemmed and rough
   chopped
1 tablespoon chaat masala

Make ahead: Rinse and soak chana dal for at least an hour, or overnight, to decrease cook time. The entire dish can be made ahead—Dal for Dummies! It will keep in the fridge for a few days, and in the freezer for up to one month.

1. Rinse soaked dal. Cover rinsed dal with water, plus one inch, in a deep saucepan. Add turmeric, salt, and pepper, and cook, covered, over medium heat to desired doneness (approximately 15 minutes; I like a little bite to the dal). Stir occasionally to keep from sticking. (Add more water if necessary.)

2. *Tadka:* Heat grapeseed oil in a deep saucepan. When oil shimmers, add mustard, fennel, and cumin seeds. (Shield yourself with a lid—the seeds pop.)

3. Add onion and jalapeño and sauté until light brown. Add garlic, cayenne flakes, and tomato. Cook for two minutes.

4. Add cooked dal and grated ginger to the *tadka.* Adjust consistency by adding water, if desired, and by pureeing a portion of the dal with a hand blender (or mashing with the back of a spoon or ladle) and returning to the pot. Check seasoning.

Crowning flavor: Top with a dollop of butter, a shower of cilantro leaves, and a sprinkle of chaat masala.

*****Disappearing Leftovers:*** Add water, Winter Squash and Pearl Onion (p. 156), or any veggie leftovers for a dal-icious soup!*

Chana dal *is high in fiber, low in fat, and very low on the glycemic index—both heart-healthy and diabetes-friendly. Although it looks like the split yellow pea, chana dal is the split kernel of a variety of garbanzo called Bengal gram and stays firmer when cooking*

Caramelized Shallots

Use shallots, red or yellow onions, or some of each—I happen to prefer the subtler, slightly sweeter flavor of shallots. Red onions will stand up to meat. This is a go-with-everything topping—veggies, grains, lentils, and meats!

YIELD: A GENEROUS ½ CUP

2 tablespoons unrefined coconut oil
4 shallots, sliced into rings
⅛ teaspoon cayenne powder
⅛ teaspoon brown sugar
½ teaspoon chaat masala
¼ teaspoon salt

Make ahead: Triple the quantities, use some, and cool and refrigerate the rest in an airtight glass jar for up to 3 days! Just warm up in a microwave or a pan before using. Caramelized shallots instantly boost the flavor of any savory dish. Slice the shallots in a food processor to save time and effort. Heat a heavy bottomed saucepan and toast seeds until fragrant, but be careful not to scorch them. It takes 2–3 minutes.

1. Heat oil in a heavy-bottomed skillet over medium heat.

2. Sauté shallots in a single layer for one minute.

3. Add the rest of the ingredients. Give a good stir and leave undisturbed until edges of the shallots start to brown. Turn shallots over and brown until golden, 4–6 minutes. Avoid burning.

DEEPA'S SECRET
My junior chef friend, Aurora Becker, suggests chewing gum to prevent tears while slicing shallots.

New Indian Gremolata

Another go-to topping, this one's inspired by the Italians. I've ditched the parsley and turned up the heat. Sprinkle it over almost any dish and every mouthful will pop with its bright, fresh flavors. Triple the quantities and keep the leftovers in the fridge.

YIELD: 1 CUP

¾ cup cilantro leaves, stemmed and finely chopped

¼ cup mint leaves, stemmed and finely chopped

2 garlic cloves, minced

2 tablespoons lemon zest

2 tablespoons fresh lemon juice

2 teaspoons jalapeño, finely chopped

½ teaspoon cumin seeds, toasted and ground

½ teaspoon fresh ground black pepper

½ teaspoon salt

1. Mix all ingredients together and top soups, grains, veggies, or meats with the New Indian Gremolata. The gremolata keeps in the fridge for up to 3 days. (Bring to room temperature before using.)

2. A drizzle (about a tablespoon) of almond oil or olive oil on top of your dish dressed with the gremolata before serving is a good idea—delicious!

Peppery Papadum

Crunchy papadum is made from non-wheat flours. Try to pick the freshest, most flexible package at your Indian store. Fried papadums only keep for a few hours—if you can get them to last that long!

Grapeseed oil, 2-inches deep in a deep 8-inch saucepan (approx. 4 cups [32 oz])

Dried papadum (plain or with cumin or black pepper)

1. Heat grapeseed oil in a deep saucepan. Drop a small corner of a dried papadum into the oil. It should turn pale yellow immediately. If it does not, wait and try again.

2. When the oil is hot enough, slide a single papadum into the oil. Immediately flip the papadum over to fry the other side (I use two forks) and quickly remove from the pan. Avoid browning the papadum, they are at their best in the pale-yellow stage! Transfer to a colander lined with paper towels. I like to stand the cooked papadum vertically in the colander, to allow excess oil to drip off.

3. If you plan to make more papadums within a couple of days (they're great appetizers and bread substitutes), you can reuse your grapeseed oil before disposing of it.

DEEPA'S SECRET

If you put the hot saucepan in the sink, avoid the disaster of getting water in the hot oil.

Gingered Farro with Dried Fruit and Nuts

Michael Pollan said, "Eat grains that your grandmother would recognize." Farro actually predates my grandmother by several thousand years—grains were found in the tombs of Egyptian kings. I have always preferred whole grains. Another secret: I used to trade lunches with my friend from the village: My fancy white bread sandwiches for her crunchy whole grain chapatis.

SERVES 4

2 cups farro
2-inch cinnamon stick

Dressing:
1 shallot, finely chopped
2 garlic cloves, minced
1 tablespoon fresh ginger, grated
1 tablespoon crystallized ginger, minced
1 tablespoon fresh lemon juice
2 tablespoons cilantro, chopped
1 teaspoon salt (or less if the cooked
    farro is already salted)

Seed mix:
2 tablespoons toasted sesame oil
½ teaspoon (Lucknow) fennel seeds
½ teaspoon cumin seeds
½ teaspoon coriander seeds
1 teaspoon sesame seeds

Dried fruit mix:
¼ teaspoon dried thyme
¼ teaspoon grated nutmeg
½ cup dried pitted Bing cherries,
    chopped
½ cup dried apricots, chopped

Crowning flavor:
1 tablespoon New Indian Gremolata
    (p. 60)
1 tablespoon Go Nuts! (p. 44) (or toasted
    sliced almonds or pine nuts)

1. Whisk dressing ingredients together in a glass bowl. Set aside.

2. Cook farro according to the package directions along with the cinnamon stick and set aside.

3. Heat oil in a 12-inch skillet and toast seed mix for a minute over medium heat. Add the dried fruit mix, stir for 30 seconds, and remove from heat.

4. Combine seed mix and dried fruit mix with farro. Mix well with dressing. Check seasoning.

5. Serve warm, and leave the cinnamon stick on top as a garnish.

Crowning flavor: Top with New Indian Gremolata. You could also add Go Nuts! (or toasted sliced almonds or toasted pine nuts).

Pairs well with Mary's Famous "Cutlets" (Meatballs) (p. 180) and Zucchini LaSuzy (p. 158) or Aviel (p. 130).

Disappearing Leftovers: Top Gingered Farro with a fried egg for a quick breakfast or a weekday meal, or freeze in individual portions for later.

Farro: You can buy farro three ways: whole, semi-pearled, and pearled. The unprocessed whole farro is the healthiest. (Note that it requires soaking overnight before cooking.) Farro has as much protein as most legumes (four times more than rice) and the high fiber content makes it gut-healthy, heart-healthy, and diabetes-friendly.

Heritage Barley (Better than Rice) Pilaf

If I could credit only one dish with getting Thampy to give up rice, this is it. It's known as "Better Than Rice Pilaf" around our house. You can eat it for breakfast, lunch, or dinner—and we do!

SERVES 6

6 cups water
2 cups whole grain barley, well-rinsed
　　and drained (I like Bob's Red Mill
　　Whole Grain Barley)

4 garlic cloves, finely chopped
1 teaspoon fennel seeds
1 teaspoon cumin seeds
2 teaspoons coriander seeds
3 cloves
2 cardamom pods
2-inch cinnamon stick
½ teaspoon salt
½ teaspoon fresh ground black pepper

Sauté vegetables:
2 tablespoons toasted sesame oil
　　(divided)
1 fennel bulb, thinly sliced
1 red bell pepper, rough chopped
1 yellow bell pepper, rough chopped
½ teaspoon salt (divided)
½ teaspoon fresh ground black pepper
　　(divided)

1 tablespoon truffle oil (optional)

Crowning flavor:
1 tablespoon fresh lemon juice
1 tablespoon New Indian Gremolata
　　(p. 60)
1 tablespoon Go Nuts! (p. 44) or toasted
　　pistachio
1 teaspoon Magic Finishing Spice (p. 28)

- -

Disappearing Leftovers: *Finely slice ¼ onion, 1 clove of garlic, and ¼ cup of cabbage. Sauté in sesame oil for a couple of minutes and add leftover barley. Top with a fried egg for a great breakfast. Heritage Barley Pilaf also freezes well.*

1. Bring 6 cups of water to a boil. Add barley, garlic, seeds, cloves, cardamom, cinnamon, salt, and pepper. Stir occasionally. Cook to desired consistency (al dente). Barley is very forgiving—just add water as needed.

2. Meanwhile, heat 1 tablespoon sesame oil in a heavy sauté pan over medium-high heat. Add fennel slices in a single layer and cook undisturbed for one minute. Turn over when lightly browned and brown the other side. Sprinkle with ¼ teaspoon salt and ¼ teaspoon pepper. Remove from heat and set aside on a platter.

3. In the same sauté pan, heat the remaining 1 tablespoon of sesame oil and add red and yellow bell peppers. Cook undisturbed over high heat for one to two minutes until lightly charred. Season with remaining ¼ teaspoon salt and ¼ teaspoon of pepper. Remove from heat and set aside on a platter.

4. Toss cooked barley with sautéed fennel and bell peppers.

5. Check seasoning and drizzle with truffle oil, if you're feeling decadent!

Crowning flavor: Top with New Indian Gremolata and Go Nuts! or toasted pistachio. A sprinkle of Magic Finishing Spice adds another flavor boost!

- -

Barley *is a whole grain with very high fiber, vitamin, mineral, and antioxidant content. Eating barley can improve your digestion and heart health, and it lowers your risk of diabetes. It has fewer calories than brown rice or quinoa.*

Pairs well with fish, meat, dal, and/or a salad. Company coming? Start with Nawabi Tuna Kebab Burger (p. 174). End with mango slices or seasonal berries on a puddle of cardamom-scented Mango Lassi (p. 194).

Kerala Quinoa

Quinoa goes native! And the Rustic Vegetable Roast adds color and flavor—quintessential Kerala!

SERVES 6

2 cups quinoa, well-rinsed and drained
   (I like red quinoa)
4 cups water

Spice mix:
2 cloves
2-inch cinnamon stick
1 bay leaf
¼ teaspoon anise seeds
¼ teaspoon coriander seeds
½ teaspoon cumin seeds
½ teaspoon fresh ground black pepper
1 teaspoon salt

Crowning flavor:
2 cups Rustic Vegetable Roast (p. 152)
2 tablespoons Caramelized Shallots
   (p. 58)
1 tablespoon Go Nuts! (p. 44) or toasted
   sliced almonds

Make ahead: Quinoa can be made 1–2 days ahead and kept in the fridge, or frozen for up to one month. Let frozen quinoa thaw overnight in the fridge and warm on the stove or in the microwave before serving.

1. Bring 4 cups of water and spice mix to a boil.

2. Add quinoa. Cook covered, on medium heat until all the water is absorbed (about 15 minutes). Allow to cool for a few minutes and check seasoning.

Crowning flavor: Before serving the quinoa, drizzle with coconut oil or top with Rustic Vegetable Roast, Caramelized Shallots, and Go Nuts! Cinnamon stick and bay leaf look good as a garnish, so I leave them in before serving family style.

On the light side? Pair with Chukku's Yogurt Salad (p. 124). Company? Pair with Tomji's Spicy Kerala Beef with Coconut Chips (p. 184) or Kerala Fisherman's Prawns (p. 172) and Crackling Okra (p. 140).

DEEPA'S SECRET

A drizzle of oil gives all cooked grains a decadent creaminess, without the cream!

Oatmeal Uppma

SERVES 6

2 cups steel cut oats

Tadka:
2 tablespoons unrefined coconut oil
½ teaspoon cumin seeds
½ teaspoon anise seed
1 teaspoon mustard seeds
1 teaspoon chana dal
1 teaspoon split urad dal
2 cloves
2-inch cinnamon stick
1 teaspoon black peppercorns, rough ground
16 curry leaves
1 jalapeño, slit into 4 pieces
1 tablespoon onion, finely chopped
2 garlic cloves, minced
½ teaspoon fresh ginger

3½ cups water
½ teaspoon asafoetida
1 teaspoon salt

1 cup green peas (frozen is fine)

Crowning flavor:
1 tablespoon fresh lemon juice
1 tablespoon cilantro leaves, stemmed and finely chopped
1 tablespoon mint leaves, stemmed and finely chopped
1 cup Spicy Snacking Peanuts (p. 46)

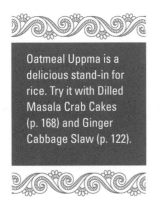

Oatmeal Uppma is a delicious stand-in for rice. Try it with Dilled Masala Crab Cakes (p. 168) and Ginger Cabbage Slaw (p. 122).

I used to use the word oatmeal synonymously with boring. It's how I described corporate America's textiles, before my designers got ahold of them. We covered Pfizer's partitions in a tone-on-tone oversized image of penicillin (they were the first distributors of the drug). Anyhow, my apologies, dear oatmeal.

Uppma is traditionally made with cream of wheat. I have made my uppma slow-carb by using steel cut oats. I halved the cooking time by dry roasting. It's even better the next day—it dries out a little and has a grainier consistency! We eat it for breakfast, and use up any leftovers with meat and vegetables at dinner.

Make ahead: Spicy Snacking Peanuts (p. 46)—this delicious snack which doubles as a topping is well worth making ahead.

1. Preheat oven to 350°F.

2. Dry roast the oats on a parchment paper-lined baking tray, for about 10 minutes, until very a light brown color with a nutty aroma. Avoid burning.

3. *Tadka*: Heat coconut oil in a 10-inch saucepan over medium heat until shimmering. Add seeds, dals, cloves, cinnamon, and black pepper—shield yourself with a lid as seeds will pop—and stir for 2 minutes. Add curry leaves, jalapeño, onion, garlic, and ginger, and sauté for one minute. Add water, asafoetida, and salt and bring to a boil.

4. Stir in roasted oats. Lower heat, cover, and simmer for 8 minutes, stirring occasionally. If oats are too firm, add ½ cup water, and simmer, covered, for 10 more minutes. Oatmeal Uppma should have a fluffy, not mushy, consistency.

5. Remove from heat, and stir in peas.

Crowning flavor: Serve topped with lemon juice, cilantro, mint, and a sprinkle of some Spicy Snacking Peanuts.

DEEPA'S SECRET
Morning breath remedy—chew on a mouthful of fennel seeds or fresh parsley.

Cinnamon can help lower cholesterol and blood sugar and is a potent anti-inflammatory agent.

"You don't thank me, silly; you go through life and you pass it on."

—Miriam Logan

6

New Beginnings

New Beginnings

iriam Logan was an unlikely surrogate mother. Mine, I mean. You can tell a lot from a photo. Miriam was Philadelphia-born Irish, gregarious, slightly raucous, and in her mid-seventies when Thampy and I became her next-door neighbors in Saratoga, California. By then, Thampy had started NexGen (a microprocessor company). Our son Suneil was four, and I was pregnant with Ahin. I hadn't had an uninterrupted night's sleep since I was pregnant the first time. There were dark days when I looked in the mirror and wondered whether my son might be better off without me.

But Miriam saw something else. She took my wrist. "Look, look around your house—look what you can do!" Back then, I had cravings. Not for food, oddly, but for beauty. I would pick flowers, sometimes weeds, and cut branches and create arrangements. I'd rearrange the furniture and every last detail of our tiny home. Thampy would tease, "Check before you sit down. Deepa may have moved your chair." The beauty lifted my spirit.

After the boys were school-aged, Miriam threw me out of my own house. She met the boys at the bus and insisted I go do something with myself.

A new beginning. One of life's greatest gifts. Even if a part of you wants to run (not walk) screaming in the other direction.

I didn't know what the hell I was going to do with myself. Miriam suggested I look into the Design Center in San Francisco, giving me a vaguely appealing description, and off I went. I studied the place, then, over the months, began to make my way into the design industry, first in residential, then corporate interiors.

Long story short, I founded Deepa Textiles. Fabric, I wouldn't expect you to know this, is the least costly element in corporate interior design. Everyone in the industry doubted I would be able to get anyone to care about it, but they underestimated how much I cared. When I imagined my fabric could change the feel of a meeting space or someone's cubicle, it sounds funny, but I knew the world was better off with me.

Larry and Miriam Logan

Miriam died the week Deepa Textiles was incorporated. Three months before she died, she called me in a panic, "Deepa, you have to help me!" Anything, I will do anything. "My hair!" She had botched her boxed dye-job.

I picked Miriam up, and hours later, my hair person made Miriam a blonde again. She couldn't stop thanking me. "Miriam, it's me, remember? How am I ever going to thank you?"

That's a long story before giving you my breakfast recipes, so I don't dare lecture you on the importance of this first meal and how skipping it throws your blood sugar levels off for the rest of the day, aside from depriving your brain (and everything else) of energy. And I won't delay you further by pointing out that people who don't eat breakfast tend to overeat throughout the rest of the day and may be more prone to diabetes, high cholesterol, etc. I'll let you get right to the recipes, since the most popular reason people don't eat breakfast is because they're strapped for time. Just one last thing, then I'll really let you go—consider a new beginning: Try becoming a breakfast-eater. I'm suggesting it for your own good, like Miriam did for mine. Now go ahead and skip directly to the recipes, unless . . .

Time isn't the issue. Perhaps you don't care much for breakfast foods, or you've been eating the wrong breakfast all along (carbs), which makes you hungry for a second breakfast* an hour later. You need protein. The recipes that follow are essentially breakfast-y, using ingredients you would expect to find in a breakfast—eggs, grains, yogurt, etc., but they're new-to-you beginnings. Then again, there are last night's leftovers. Any vegetable or grain recipe in this book can be warmed up and topped with an egg or two for a super-quick, super-satisfying start to your day. Nothing in the definition of the word breakfast says you can't—you're breaking the fast. Nothing more. Nothing less.

*A quick note here about the second breakfast, (and I'll come back to this story in Chapter 13), aka snacking: I lost those twenty pounds and have kept them off by eating four or five small meals a day. Keeping my hunger at bay by eating more often (more slowly and less ravenously), I actually consumed fewer calories overall, not that I ever counted them. There's nothing wrong with a second breakfast, as long as you're not sabotaging your pancreas. Consider the old "eat when you're hungry, but not too hungry" maxim, modified. You want to avoid big swings in your blood sugar levels, which affect insulin production. Plan on two snacks (a couple handfuls of nuts, fruits, or vegetables) and lunch to tide you over to dinner.

Masala Omelet

"Masala omelet please, Krishnan?" Our family cook made my breakfast every morning. I loved to watch him froth the egg with a fork, and then he'd tuck deep-fried cream-soaked bread in the middle—yum! Sorry, not included here. (It takes a lot to get a teenager out of bed.)

SERVES 2

2 tablespoons extra virgin olive or unrefined coconut oil
2 cups parsley, stemmed and rough
chopped
2 shallots, finely chopped
1 jalapeño, minced
1 clove garlic, minced
¼ teaspoon cayenne flakes
Salt and fresh ground black pepper, to
taste
4 eggs, whisked with a fork until frothy

1. Heat oil in a 12-inch nonstick sauté pan over medium heat. Shield yourself with a lid as you toss in the chopped parsley, as it will splutter before it crisps up. Now lower the heat and add shallots. Sauté until light brown in color, about 5 minutes. Add jalapeño, garlic, cayenne flakes, salt, and pepper to the pan and sauté for 30 seconds.

2. Pour the beaten eggs into the pan, lower the heat to the lowest setting, cover, and cook (do not stir) until done, about 2 minutes. Loosen from the pan with a spatula and fold in half.

3. Top with Caramelized Shallots (p. 58) for a punchy crunch.

Jalapeño and Dill Scramble

We had dill seed, but not dill weed when I grew up in India. This combination is one of my guys' favorite breakfasts. (I still have a soft spot for the original favorite, boy-made "pizza" muffins: Thomas's (!) English muffins and cheddar, dotted with ketchup. Lots of ketchup.)

SERVES 2

1 tablespoon unrefined coconut oil
1 jalapeño, chopped
1 tablespoon fresh dill, chopped
   (or ½ tablespoon dried)
½ garlic clove, grated
Salt and fresh ground black pepper,
   to taste
4 eggs, whisked

2 sprigs dill, for garnish

1. Heat oil in an 8-inch nonstick skillet over medium heat. Add all ingredients (except the dill sprigs).

2. Gently fold in the eggs with a rubber spatula (1½ minutes), lower the heat, and cook to preferred doneness.

3. Garnish with sprigs of dill and enjoy immediately.

DEEPA'S SECRET
If you like big curds of egg (like I do), fold the mixture from the sides of the pan to the center until curds form. Reduce heat and allow curds to cook until done.

Tofu and Asparagus Scramble

1973 is the year when A) tofu was invented; B) tofu was introduced to America; C) *I first tried tofu*; D) the mood ring was patented. I had tofu in Chinese food soon after I arrived in America. Now that I have two vegetarian daughters-in-law, tofu is a Thomas kitchen staple. I prefer the medium firm tofu, patted dry. Gotta love the protein!

SERVES 2

2 tablespoons toasted sesame oil
3 eggs, beaten
1 cup tofu, finely chopped
2 cups asparagus, sliced into ¼-inch
    pieces
1 shallot, finely chopped
1 teaspoon soy sauce
1 teaspoon sriracha
1 tablespoon cilantro, stemmed and
    finely chopped
Salt and fresh ground black pepper, to
    taste

Crowning flavor:
1 tablespoon Go Nuts! (p. 44)

1. Heat oil in a nonstick skillet over medium heat. Add the beaten eggs with the rest of the ingredients at once and let set for 30 seconds.

2. Use a ladle or rubber spatula to pull the egg from the edges to the middle of the pan in long sweeps to form fluffy "curds." Lower heat and cook to desired doneness.

Crowning flavor: Sprinkle Go Nuts! on top for a savory flavor boost.

Asparagus: *This slim stalk is long on nutrients, antioxidants, and the amino acid asparagine, which is a diuretic. The release of fluids also rids the body of excess salt, which helps control high blood pressure and heart disease.*

Fried Eggs on a Bed of Cabbage

This recipe is a great breakfast of leftovers. It also makes a nice, light dinner. If you have leftovers or make some Hot 'n' Crispy Cabbage (p. 150) or Caramelized Shallots (p. 58) ahead, your bed will already be made! I like to top my eggs with New Indian Gremolata. I always have a jarful on the door in the fridge.

SERVES 1

1 tablespoon unrefined coconut oil
1 green or red chili, slit into 4 with the
    top intact
4 curry leaves
2 eggs
Salt and fresh ground pepper, to taste

Crowning flavor:
1 tablespoon New Indian Gremolata
    (p. 60)

1. Heat oil in a 6-inch skillet over medium heat. Add chili and cook for one minute, just to flavor the oil. Add the curry leaves (don't forget to use a lid to shield yourself from spluttering).

2. Fry eggs in oil to desired doneness. Season with salt and pepper.

3. In a separate pan, or in the microwave, warm Caramelized Shallots or Hot 'n' Crispy Cabbage or any leftover vegetables or grains. Top with fried eggs.

Crowning flavor: Garnish with New Indian Gremolata.

Eggs: *They're good again. Study after study has shown that any rise in bad cholesterol is offset by a rise in good cholesterol. Eggs pack a protein punch (after all, they were designed to grow a chick) and are loaded with vitamins and minerals.*

Sprouted Mung Beans on Egg Salad

My mom always kept a jar of sprouted beans in the fridge. They are a bit labor-intensive, but they were my dad's favorite snack. He had us all trained—a bowlful, tossed with lemon juice, a little chopped onion, jalapeño, cilantro, and a fork, please and thank you.

SERVES 6

1 cup sprouted mung beans

Seasoning mix:
½ yellow onion, finely chopped
1 jalapeño, seeded and finely chopped
1 garlic clove, minced
1 teaspoon fresh ginger, minced
1 tablespoon mint leaves, stemmed and
 finely chopped
1 tablespoon fresh cilantro, stemmed
 and finely chopped
½ teaspoon *jal jeera* powder (available
 in Indian grocery stores or online)
1 tablespoon fresh lemon juice
1 teaspoon salt
½ teaspoon fresh ground black pepper

6 eggs

Flavor mix:
1 teaspoon sweet pickle relish
1 tablespoon extra virgin olive oil
½ teaspoon chaat masala
¼ teaspoon cayenne powder

Edible flower petals (optional)

Make ahead: It will take your mung beans about 36 hours to swell and sprout. Put rinsed mung beans (sprout extra for snacking!) in a bowl and cover with cold water. Leave at room temperature. After 24 hours, drain the water and wrap the beans in a double layer of cheese cloth. Place the covered beans on a large plate or baking sheet and leave at room temperature. Keep the cheese cloth damp. The beans will sprout in twelve hours. Store your sprouted mung beans in a lidded glass container in the fridge for up to a week.

1. Stir seasoning mix into the sprouted mung beans.

2. Place 6 eggs in a deep saucepan with enough water to just cover the eggs. Bring to a boil over medium heat, lower the heat, and boil gently for 1 minute. Cover the pan and turn off the heat. Let cool for 10 minutes. Rinse and peel eggs in cold water, then slice and arrange on a platter.

3. Whip the flavor mix with a fork and drizzle onto sliced eggs.

4. Top sliced eggs with sprouted mung bean mixture. An edible flower petal garnish adds a colorful touch!

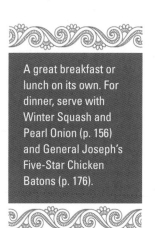

A great breakfast or lunch on its own. For dinner, serve with Winter Squash and Pearl Onion (p. 156) and General Joseph's Five-Star Chicken Batons (p. 176).

Mung beans have been one of the most cherished foods in traditional Ayurvedic cuisine for thousands of years. They are just beginning to show up here in American cooking. The little green beans are dense with nutrients, protein, and fiber, and they have antioxidant, anti-inflammatory, anti-diabetic, and anti-hypertensive effects. The sprouted beans are low-calorie and very filling. Great snack food.

Red, White, and Blue Berry Breakfast Salad

My small homage to this great country of ours. Thampy and I just earned our citizenship in 2012. The ceremony is one I believe every American should experience. Twelve hundred of us were sworn in. We each stood when the State department official thanked us in Hindi for choosing America—*shukriya*, a formal thank you. And we watched proudly while he did the same for the others, in their native languages, 140 countries in all. Proud of ourselves, proud of our fellow new citizens, proud of these United States of America.

SERVES 2

Yogurt mixture:
2 cups plain Greek yogurt
⅛ teaspoon ground cardamom
¼ teaspoon vanilla extract
1 teaspoon wild honey
Salt and fresh ground black pepper,
   to taste

½ cup raspberries
½ cup blackberries
½ cup blueberries
½ cup strawberries, sliced

Crowning flavor:
¼ cup Go Nuts! (p. 44)

1. Stir yogurt mixture well in a glass bowl. Check seasoning.

2. Pool yogurt on individual plates or serve in a bowl, topped with berries.

Crowning flavor: Add a sprinkle of Go Nuts! for extra crunch, flavor, and nutrients!

Berries: blueberries, strawberries, and blackberries are bursting with antioxidants and fiber. The anthocyanins (the red and blue pigments) in strawberries and blueberries have been linked to the prevention of cognitive decline. And, with their fiber content, berries are diabetes-friendly. Sweet!

DEEPA'S SECRET
This "breakfast" is also my go-to dessert with a shaving of dark chocolate on top.

> *"Food is meant to be shared."*
> —My mother, *Amma*, Mary *Sosamma* Thomas Mathew

7

Soups and Stews

Soups and Stews

Leftovers + broth = soup, ta da!

I'll begin by sharing this: My mother and I had an adversarial relationship, but I can thankfully say it ended in a truce. (*Amma*'s been gone more than fifteen years now.) It took me some time, and perhaps having children of my own, to (in this order) realize, understand, and respect that my mother, like the rest of us, was doing her best.

As the mother of two sons I can't say for sure, but I like to think today's mothers are more aware and sensitive to their daughters' body images than mine was back in the early 1960s. *Amma* openly despaired during my pudgy tween years, and her "best" contributed to a lifelong pudgy-pendulum. (I did my first thirty-day diet aka starvation diet before I was seventeen.) On the flip side, some of my best memories of *Amma* have to do with food.

Mary Mathew, as the rest of the world knew her, was a 1950s career woman. A Montessori-trained teacher, she taught Indira Gandhi's children. And later in her administrative role at New Delhi's YWCA, my mother welcomed the Queen of England on her first visit to India. In her spare time, *Amma* was a gardener, with a thriving canopy of grapevines and a stunning rose garden in the backyard, and she was an accomplished amateur baker.

Amma also presided over our evening "teas," which were set under the Neem (Indian Lilac) tree. No Mathew family tea service was complete without a surprise guest, or three or four. As a kid, I would have sworn to you that *Amma*'s refrigerator was magic. At week's end, when we were running low on groceries, I'd follow her to the fridge and peer in when she swung open the door. Every time, she'd pull out a plate of something perfectly sweet, or savory, and those bites would tide our guests over until her much-anticipated meat "cutlets" (p. 180) arrived at the table. The cutlets were pulled out of some other secret compartment, already made up and ready to fry, accompanied by ice-cold Taj Mahal beer. (No mystery there, my dad kept the bottom shelf perpetually stocked.)

Amma never passed her fridge magic on to me, and Annapurna herself (the goddess of nourishment) knows I could have used it when my boys were teens,

My mother, Mary *Sosamma* Thomas Mathew

but I do have a couple of tricks I will share with you. First, in this chapter, you have the recipes for my go-to soups and stews—the Old Indian standards updated, and some clever (if I do say so) newcomers. But, you also have the makings for countless soups of your own creation: leftovers + broth = soup, *ta da!* Want more stews? Take any soup, puree about a quarter—don't add anything (no flour, no corn starch)—just put it back in the pot, check the salt and pepper, and *presto change-o*, you've got stew!

There is no misunderstanding: food, its preparation, or sometimes the simple act of serving it, equals love. It warms our insides, fills us up. Just the thought, let alone the sight and aroma, of a big pot simmering on the stove is, without a doubt, comforting. (I claimed that we "eat" with our eyes first; perhaps I should amend that to our eyes and our noses!) However, our relationship with food has the potential to rival our relationships with our mothers in their complexity. Food is not a substitute for love, and no amount, unfortunately, can fill a certain kind of hole or emptiness.

Not unrelated, I have had an adversarial relationship with food perpetuated by years of the wrong kind of dieting. Some therapy and, ironically, cooking, especially this conscious cooking, has resolved it. Think about it: food is hardly a worthy adversary. Some moms might be able to go a few rounds with a gladiator, but food? Doesn't stand a chance. You can control food. Everything you make, every bite you take . . . try to love (okay, I'll settle for *like*) yourself with food.

Tomato Rasam

This soup is also known as the Thomas's "sniffle-kicking" soup. There's enough garlic in a bowlful to kill a cold, and several vampires . . . The pepper, asafoetida, cumin, turmeric, and tomato will help clear up any inflammation in the sinuses. Leftover soup or this future cold remedy will keep in the freezer for up to a month.

SERVES 4

Roasted tomato-onion mixture:
12 ripe tomatoes, whole
½ onion, rough chopped
1 tablespoon unrefined coconut oil, melted over low heat

Tadka:
¼ cup sesame oil
2 teaspoons split urad dal
2 teaspoons brown mustard seeds
2 teaspoons cumin seeds
2 whole dried cayennes, rough crushed
12 curry leaves

Fresh spice blend:
3 tablespoons fresh ginger, peeled and rough chopped
10 garlic cloves, smashed with a mallet or a flat knife
3 tablespoons black peppercorns, smashed or rough ground
2 teaspoons salt

Ground spices:
¼ teaspoon turmeric
½ teaspoon cumin seeds, toasted and ground
½ teaspoon ground fenugreek
1 teaspoon asafoetida

1 cup cilantro leaves (divided, save half for garnish)

3 cups water

Crowning flavor:
1 tablespoon fresh lemon juice
½ teaspoon chaat masala
½ cup cucumber, chopped

1. Preheat oven to 375°F. Line a baking tray with parchment paper. Spread tomatoes and chopped onion in a single layer. Drizzle with coconut oil. Roast for 20 minutes.

2. *Tadka:* Heat sesame oil in a soup pot. When the oil starts shimmering, add urad dal. As it starts to brown (about 30 seconds), add mustard and cumin seeds. Shield yourself with a lid as seeds will start popping immediately. Add dried cayennes and curry leaves.

3. Add the fresh spice blend, ground spices, and half the cilantro leaves. Sauté for one minute or until fragrant.

4. Add the roasted tomato-onion mixture and water, and simmer uncovered for 15 minutes. Remove from heat. Check seasoning. Blend to a broth consistency (add more water, if needed). Heat well before serving.

Crowning flavor: Stir lemon juice and chaat masala into the rasam. Ladle the rasam into pretty teacups. Garnish with chopped cucumber and the remaining cilantro leaves.

Ladle into a teacup with a sprinkle of Caramelized Shallots (p. 58) for a Wow! starter. Then serve Tomji's Spicy Kerala Beef with Coconut Chips (p. 184) and a cool side of Chukku's Yogurt Salad (p. 124).

Almost five thousand years ago, Charak, the father of Ayurvedic medicine, declared that garlic "strengthens the heart and keeps blood fluid." In the West, within the last ten years, a similar declaration has been made: garlic protects against atherosclerosis, or the clogging of arteries. Garlic can lower cholesterol, blood pressure, blood sugar, fight infection and yes, the common cold.

New Indian Pesto and Bean Soup

I couldn't resist a reinterpretation of the Italian classic. Totally and wonderfully different.

SERVES 4

3 cups cilantro, rough chopped

3 cups mint leaves, stemmed and rough chopped

2 cups basil leaves, stemmed and rough chopped

1 tablespoon dried thyme

1 medium onion, rough chopped

3 garlic cloves, chopped

1 sundried tomato, sliced into thin strips

1 cup pine nuts

1 teaspoon anise seeds

½ teaspoon cayenne flakes

¼ teaspoon allspice

6 cups water

1 teaspoon salt

½ teaspoon fresh ground black pepper

2 cans (15 oz) cannellini (or your favorite) beans, drained and rinsed well

2 tablespoons extra virgin olive oil

Make ahead: You can make New Indian Pesto and Bean Soup ahead of time and store it in the fridge for a couple of days, or freeze in individual servings and defrost in a flash.

1. Puree all ingredients except beans and olive oil in a blender.

2. Bring the puree to a simmer in a deep saucepan. Add beans. Lower heat and cook uncovered for 5 minutes.

3. Remove from heat. Check seasoning and drizzle olive oil over each bowl of soup before serving.

Disappearing Leftovers: For a great side dish, add a cup of soup to 2 cups of stir-fried veggies of your choice.

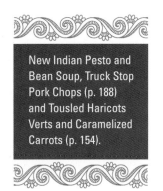

New Indian Pesto and Bean Soup, Truck Stop Pork Chops (p. 188) and Tousled Haricots Verts and Caramelized Carrots (p. 154).

Roasted Cauliflower Soup

This is a real comfort soup. The toasted almonds on top of the creamy cream-free soup are a throwback to the cups of steamed milk our neighbor's grandmother served us when we were kids. She'd soak her almonds in milk overnight, then grind them with the milk, which she warmed and ladled into cups for us to drink. Instant milk moustaches!

SERVES 6

Roasted cauliflower:
1 large whole cauliflower, cut into florets, then sliced about ¼-inch thick
½ teaspoon cayenne powder
½ teaspoon turmeric
½ teaspoon dried thyme
½ teaspoon salt
2 tablespoons unrefined coconut oil (melted over low heat)

Broth:
2 tablespoons unrefined coconut oil
1 tablespoon butter
1 onion, sliced
3 garlic cloves, thinly sliced
1 tablespoon grated ginger
8 curry leaves
¼ teaspoon ground cloves
¼ teaspoon ground cardamom
4 cups broth (*Sosamma*'s Basic Broth [p. 52] or any low-sodium broth)

Crowning flavor:
2 hard-boiled eggs, grated
½ cup sliced almonds, toasted
1 tablespoon chives, minced

1. Preheat oven to 400ºF, position rack in the middle of the oven.

2. Line a baking tray with parchment paper and arrange the cauliflower slices in a single layer. Sprinkle with cayenne powder, turmeric, thyme and salt. Drizzle with 2 tablespoons of coconut oil and roast for 20 minutes.

3. In the meantime, heat coconut oil and butter in a wide saucepan. Add onion. Lower the temperature, cover, and cook, stirring occasionally until soft, about 10 minutes.

4. Add garlic, ginger, curry leaves, cloves, and cardamom. Shield yourself with a lid as curry leaves could splutter. Sauté for one minute. Add broth. Simmer until cauliflower in the oven is done, about 10 minutes.

5. Add roasted cauliflower to broth, reserving a few slices for garnish. Puree soup with handheld or regular blender. Check seasoning.

Crowning flavor: Serve each bowl of soup topped with slices of roasted cauliflower and grated eggs, sliced almonds, and chives.

Follow Roasted Cauliflower Soup with Mary's Famous "Cutlets" (Meatballs) (p. 180) and Hot 'n' Crispy Cabbage (p. 150).

Cauliflower is a very low-glycemic food, which can be eaten in quantity without destabilizing blood sugar levels. It is also a great gut food, with heart health, brain health, and antioxidant benefits.

Herbed Asparagus and Macadamia Soup

The macadamia nut was my father's favorite nut. A bagful was an exotic treat from America until they started growing them in India. Macadamia nuts give this asparagus soup a nice velvety texture. A few nuts, rough chopped, make a beautiful garnish.

SERVES 2

Sauté ingredients:
1 bunch (8–10 stalks) asparagus
2 tablespoons extra virgin olive oil
1 shallot, rough chopped
1 garlic clove, smashed
1 leek, rough chopped
1 jalapeño, chopped (remove seeds for less heat)
½ teaspoon salt
½ teaspoon fresh ground black pepper

Simmer ingredients:
1 teaspoon fresh ginger, grated
¼ teaspoon caraway seeds
½ teaspoon fresh thyme leaves (or ¼ teaspoon dried)
½ teaspoon dried savory
1 bay leaf
1 quart chicken or vegetable broth (*Sosamma*'s Basic Broth [p. 52] or low sodium prepared)
1 teaspoon butter (optional)

¾ cup roasted and salted macadamia nuts, rough chopped (save ¼ cup for topping)

Crowning flavor:
1 tablespoon fresh lemon juice
½ teaspoon toasted black sesame seeds

1. Peel asparagus stalks with a vegetable peeler. Snap off and discard the ends of the asparagus stalks. Save the tips for garnish. Rough chop the stalks.

2. Heat oil in a deep 8-inch saucepan. Add the sauté ingredients. Stir, lower heat, and sauté for 5 minutes to soften, but do not brown.

3. Add the simmer ingredients (including the broth). Simmer for 5 minutes, careful not to boil!

4. Cool slightly, add macadamia nuts (save some for garnish) and blend, using a regular blender or a hand blender. Add more broth or water if your soup is too thick. Return to saucepan and heat through.

Crowning flavor: Stir in lemon juice. Check seasoning. Serve warm. Garnish the individual soup bowls with reserved asparagus tips (blanched in salt water or raw), reserved chopped macadamia nuts, and toasted sesame seeds.

Macadamia nut: *It's a super nut! An excellent source of the rare omega-7 palmitoleic acid, which has the ability to control diabetes, speed the metabolism of fat, and protect brain nerve cells.*

Herbed Asparagus and Macadamia Soup, followed by New Indian Cacciatore (p. 178), Crackling Okra (p. 140), and Gingered Farro with Dried Fruit and Nuts (p. 64).

Mamamimi's 'Shroom Soup

Mamamimi, as the boys called her, took liberties with her recipes. Her "potassium" (doctor's orders) was OJ and vodka on the rocks. Her mushroom soup consisted of the mushrooms she loved with the cream she loved even more. This is a creamy mushroom soup (not a mushroomy cream soup) that doesn't call for cream. Inspired by our dear friend Miriam, I can practically hear her saying, "Everything calls for cream, dear."

SERVES 4

3 tablespoons sesame oil

3 shallots, minced

1 teaspoon garlic paste (3 cloves, ground to a paste in a food processor)

½ teaspoon ginger paste (¼-inch ginger, ground to a paste in a food processor)

½ teaspoon cayenne flakes

20 shiitake mushrooms, sliced

½ teaspoon salt

½ teaspoon fresh ground black pepper

¼ cup water or white wine

2 teaspoons fresh thyme leaves

¼ teaspoon allspice

1 tablespoon fresh lemon juice

1 quart broth, chicken or vegetarian *Sosamma*'s Basic Broth (p. 52) or low sodium prepared

Crowning flavor:

1 cup fresh parsley, stemmed and rough chopped

1. Heat oil in a heavy 12-inch saucepan over medium heat. Add shallots and sauté until golden brown, about 5 minutes. Set aside half the caramelized shallots as a topping for later on.

2. Add garlic and ginger pastes and cayenne flakes to the sauté pan. Stir for 30 seconds until fragrant.

3. Add mushrooms and toss once. Wait a couple of minutes, add salt and pepper, and give another stir.

4. Cook until mushrooms develop brown edges (about 5–8 minutes), then add wine or water. Loosen brown bits and stir until liquid is evaporated. Add thyme and allspice. Stir well, remove from heat, and add lemon juice. If you like, save a little bit of mushroom sauté for your egg breakfast tomorrow.

5. To make this deliciousness into soup, blend half the mushrooms with broth into a rough, rustic consistency. Heat and top with the remaining sautéed mushrooms and check seasoning.

Crowning flavor: Top the individual serving bowls of soup with the caramelized shallots (that were set aside in step 1) and chopped parsley.

Disappearing leftovers: Toss some cooked whole grain pasta with the leftover soup as a sauce!

Start with *Mamamimi*'s 'Shroom Soup and finish with Chop Chop Lamb Chops (p. 182) and Roasted Beets and Shaved Fennel Salad (p. 110).

Shiitakes are the second most popular mushroom in the world. They are full of vitamins B and D, and they have the ability to boost heart health and the immune system. They also help to control blood sugar.

Meat Lovers' Indian Chili

Perfect for a Sunday supper, or an afternoon football party. Cricket is the national pastime in India. (My mother was addicted to the sport.) The spreads at cricket parties were unbelievable—an American football party times three—and the grazing was nonstop.

SERVES 6

1 cup canned kidney beans, drained and rinsed well
½ cup canned black beans, drained and rinsed well

Bean flavor pack:
1 teaspoon cumin seeds
½ teaspoon anise seeds
1 teaspoon coriander seeds
1 tablespoon salt

Onion-celery mix (finely chopped or pulsed in food processor):
1 cup onion
1 cup celery
1 cup carrot
6 cloves garlic

2 slices bacon (preferably hickory-smoked), chopped
2 tablespoons extra virgin olive oil
1 lb ground sirloin
½ pound ground pork (or more ground beef)

Meat flavor pack:
1 tablespoon paprika
1–2 teaspoons cayenne powder
¼ teaspoon ground cloves
1 tablespoon cumin seeds, toasted and ground
1 teaspoon Herbs de Provence
1 teaspoon dried oregano
2 teaspoons chili powder
1 teaspoon granulated garlic and parsley
1 teaspoon dried thyme
2 tablespoons tomato paste
1 can (14 oz) chopped tomatoes
2 cups water
1 teaspoon salt

Crowning flavor:
½ cup onion, finely chopped
2 cups Jalapeño Monterey Jack or favorite cheese, grated
2 tablespoons fresh lemon juice

Make ahead: You can make this chili up to two days ahead of time—it not only keeps, but improves, as the flavors meld, with age—so you can sit back and enjoy the game.

1. Drain beans and put into a heavy 10-quart pot. Add bean flavor pack, half of the onion-celery mix, and enough fresh water to cover beans by about an inch. Cook, covered, over medium heat, stirring occasionally, for about 15 minutes.

2. Meanwhile, brown bacon in another large pot (10–12 quart). Add 2 tablespoons of olive oil and the remaining half of onion-celery mix. Sauté over medium heat for about 8 minutes. Add meat and brown (about 8 minutes), breaking up any lumps of ground sirloin.

3. Add meat flavor pack, and cook for another 8 minutes, stirring occasionally.

4. Mix cooked beans into meat and cook for another 15 minutes, stirring occasionally. Add water if you like a soupier chili and heat thoroughly. Check seasoning.

Crowning flavor: Serve with chopped onions and grated cheese with a fresh squeeze of lemon juice on top.

Serve with Peppery Papadum (p. 62) and a side of Best-Ever Oven-Roasted Swee' Potato Fries (p. 132).

Mix leftover chili with cooked quinoa pasta for a quick lunch or dinner.

"*No one is one degree superior to you.
No one is one degree inferior to you.*"

—My father, *Dada*, Dr. N. T. Mathew

8

Salad Days

Salad Days

There was one midday meal—I must've been nine or ten—when I dropped my salad fork. I peered down at it, then called out to the kitchen, "I need a new fork, please."

My dad put his fork down. "Deepa," he said. Our eyes locked. "Are your legs broken?"

I was out of my chair and in the silverware drawer in a *jaldi* flash! He never had to ask again.

My dad was Director General of Indian Statistics in India's Central Government. In his position, he oversaw a staff of thousands, including one Gajan Singh. Gajan Singh was employed, among other things, to carry my dad's briefcase, and I think the fact of it made my dad uncomfortable; after all, his arms weren't broken. But as he explained it to me, "If I carry my briefcase, I will be depriving Gajan Singh of a job." My dad, generally a man of few words, came to know the man very well after all of their walks from his desk to his car together. And for as long as we knew of their whereabouts, my dad looked in on the Singhs.

Pretense was just about the only character trait my dad couldn't tolerate. And given his intellectual bandwidth, he had a well-developed, wide-ranging detector. In addition to being a numbers guy, my dad read to us from Plato and Socrates, knew Russian fairy tales inside and out, and was still able to recite Lincoln's Gettysburg Address in its entirety when he was eighty-six.

On the face of it, *Dada* was a traditional father. I heard my share of *because I said so*'s. But unlike other New Delhi dads at the time, my father's expectations of (and for) his two little girls were the same as those of his son. We were schooled in debate (aka not taking *no* for an answer) at the dinner table. And while my mother-the-teacher gave up on my academic abilities when I brought home less-than-stellar grades in elementary school, my dad recognized I learned differently and tasked himself with teaching me math visually.

My dad truly believed each of us could be or do anything. He never went on about any of us—in fact, quite the opposite—so a rare compliment from *Dada* was that much more powerful. Praise, transformative. And while my mom felt comfortable telling the world what to do (and was, I have to admit, mostly right), we had to ask my dad for advice. "A thirsty horse comes to water," he'd say with a half-smile.

Dada

I inherited my dad's belief-gene and his anti-prescriptive (MYOB) tendencies. And my sixty-some years of life experience have strengthened both. When I suggest you can lose weight or self-regulate your blood sugar, I want to preface it by saying, "If *I* can do it, then . . . " And, instead of giving you a diet, I am giving you choices. Lots of tasty, healthy choices.

Whether you eat your salad *before* or *after* your main course has been a matter of cultural or personal preference. It may also have metabolic consequences— some evidence suggests that vinegar moderates spikes in blood sugar levels. When you make your salad the main, you're making an undebatable difference. The rawer your ingredients, the more work your body does breaking them down and the better it is for you—it's a difference you will actually feel (if you pay attention).

Test it out: try any one of these recipes (or a low-carb kitchen sink salad of your own devising) for lunch, then monitor your energy level and productivity after lunch. Compare that with your energy level and productivity after a sandwich, burrito, a couple slices of pizza, your regular lunch, or no lunch at all.

You could take it a step further: I am not a fan of the various "cleanses." A little too punishing to the body,

not to mention the wallet. But I have been known to jolt my metabolism and shed a few pounds of creepage with "salad days." String three or four days together when you simply have nothing but salad for one (dinner), two, three, or all five small meals.

To cut down on your meal prep time, do yourself a favor and wash the greens when you bring them home. Wrap them in paper towels and store in Ziploc bags in the fridge. And, have a favorite salad dressing or two made up ahead of time. The recipes in this chapter are micronutrient-rich, simple to prepare, beautiful to plate (if that's your thing), and incredibly satisfying to eat. Each can be made ahead of time and keep very well in the fridge.

My dad might wrinkle his brow, seeing himself at the helm of this chapter. He loved his raw veggies, but he was also famous family-wide for saying, "Now that I've had my diet food, I'd like my real food." (Incidentally, I used that quote as a litmus test for the recipes in this book—anything that tasted like diet food ended up in the garbage disposal!) *Dada*'s love provided much of the substance and sustenance of my "salad days." These days, I can't ask his advice, but, strange as it may sound, I can still learn from him. I just ask myself: "What would *Dada* do?"

Deepaganoush on Endive

Belgian endive hadn't made it to New Delhi before I left in 1973. I first tasted it at a design industry reception in the eighties. I like the sharp flavor, and I love the way the little boats cup the ingredients.

SERVES 6

2 medium eggplants, charred

3 tablespoons extra virgin olive oil
½ red onion, finely chopped
3 garlic cloves, minced
1 jalapeño, seeds removed for less heat and finely chopped

Dried spices:
2 teaspoons cumin seeds, toasted and ground
1 teaspoon turmeric
¼ teaspoon fennel powder
½ teaspoon allspice
½ teaspoon cayenne powder
½ teaspoon paprika
½ teaspoon salt
¼ teaspoon fresh ground black pepper

1 small can (6 oz) tomatoes, chopped
1-inch piece fresh ginger, peeled and minced
2 tablespoons fresh lemon juice
12–24 endive leaves

Crowning flavor:
1 teaspoon chaat masala
3 tablespoons fresh cilantro, stemmed and finely chopped
2 tablespoons chives, finely chopped

Make ahead: Prepare the eggplant (steps 1–2) the day before. It will keep in the fridge overnight until you are ready to fill the endive leaves.

1. Use tongs to char eggplants over a gas burner. (Or, place on a tray in a preheated 450ºF oven for 20–30 minutes until skin is blackened). Place charred eggplants in a glass bowl and cover with foil for 10 minutes to release the skin, then peel. A bit messy, but worth the effort!

2. Heat oil in a large sauté pan over medium heat. Add onion and sauté until soft, about 3 minutes. Add garlic and jalapeño and stir for 30 seconds. Add all the dried spices and stir until fragrant, about one minute (careful not to burn!). Add tomatoes and fresh ginger, cover, and cook for one minute. Add charred eggplant and lemon juice and mix well. Then lower heat, cover, and cook for 10 minutes. Check seasoning. (The charred eggplant filling can be blended smooth or left in chunks and will keep in the fridge overnight. Bring it to room temperature before you fill the endive leaves.)

3. Fill endive leaves with the charred eggplant filling.

Crowning flavor: Sprinkle chaat masala, chopped cilantro, and chives on top of filled endive leaves.

Serve Deepaganoush on Endive as an appetizer alongside Quick Chana Masala (p. 134), Chukku's Yogurt Salad (p. 124), and Keema Spicy Beef (p. 186).

Eggplant: The Hindi word for eggplant is baingan, *meaning without merit. Actually, the high-fiber, low-carb vegetable has been used to control diabetes for centuries. Provided it isn't fried (eggplants soak up fat), eggplant is heart-healthy, and can lower cholesterol and blood pressure.*

Roasted Beets and Shaved Fennel Salad

We ate tons of beets growing up. When roasted, they tasted like candy! I never had to suffer the ones that came out of a can; there was no canned food to be had in New Delhi. Nor was there fresh fennel, but it tastes a lot like anise, which is a very familiar flavor. I've had a lot of taste memories since I started eating more consciously—turns out you can be here and there at the same time now.

SERVES 4

4 small red beets
6 small yellow beets
1 teaspoon salt
½ teaspoon fresh ground black pepper

Whipped yogurt:
1 cup Greek yogurt, whipped with a
    hand blender
1 teaspoon wild orange honey
½ teaspoon salt
¼ teaspoon fresh ground black pepper

¼ teaspoon fennel seeds, toasted and
    ground
¼ teaspoon cumin seeds, toasted and
    ground

1 cup fennel, thinly sliced or shaved
    (save a few fennel fronds for a
    garnish)
1 teaspoon fresh lemon juice

Crowning flavor:
3 tablespoons extra virgin olive oil
½ teaspoon chaat masala
1 cup pistachios, lightly toasted, rough
    chopped

Serve Roasted Beets
and Shaved Fennel
Salad with Nawabi
Tuna Kebab Burger
(p. 174) and Ralph's
Garlicky Spinach a la
Dal (p. 142).

1. Preheat oven to 400°F. Wrap the beets (I like to wrap them individually but you could put them together) in foil and roast for 40–45 minutes, until tender. Cool to room temperature. Peel and cut roasted beets into segments. Season with salt and pepper.

2. While the beets are in the oven, combine yogurt, honey, salt, and pepper together with a whisk. Check seasoning and set aside.

3. Pool the whipped yogurt on a salad plate (should extend to 1-inch from the edge of the plate). Sprinkle the yogurt with toasted and ground fennel and cumin.

4. Slice the fennel as thinly as possible. Immediately toss the slices with lemon juice to prevent them from turning brown.

5. Arrange a generous pile of beet segments on the salad plate with the pool of yogurt. Top with fennel slices and fronds.

Crowning flavor: Drizzle with olive oil, dust with chaat masala, and top with a shower of chopped pistachios.

Fennel, Radicchio, and Fresh Berry Salad

You say *tomato* and I say *tomahto*. You say *radicchio*, I say, I thought my pronunciation woes were behind me once I mastered *soliloquy* and the silent *h* in *heir*. The slightly bitter note of however-you-say *radicchio* sets off the sweet berries. A satisfying explosion of color and flavor!

SERVES 4

Dressing:
1 clove garlic, minced
½ teaspoon garam masala
½ teaspoon cayenne flakes
½ teaspoon maple syrup
1 teaspoon tamarind paste, diluted in
    ½ cup water
1 tablespoon dill (fresh, chopped) or
    ½ tablespoon dried
½ cup extra virgin olive oil
1 tablespoon apricot or your favorite
    fruit vinegar
3 tablespoons fresh lemon juice
1 teaspoon salt
½ teaspoon fresh ground black pepper

Salad ingredients:
1 fennel bulb, thinly sliced
1 large radicchio, leaves separated
1 shallot, finely chopped
1 plum or apple, thinly sliced
1 cup mixed berries
1 cup cucumber, thinly sliced
½ red onion, thinly sliced
1 cup cherry tomatoes, halved
1 cup baby spinach or baby lettuce
    leaves

Crowning flavor:
Zest of 2 lemons, for garnish
1 cup toasted sliced almonds
1 teaspoon chaat masala

1. Whisk together dressing ingredients in a glass bowl. Check seasoning and set aside.

2. Arrange salad ingredients (like you would flowers) on a large platter.

3. Drizzle the dressing over the salad.

Crowning flavor: Garnish the salad with lemon zest. If you're feeling nutty, top with a handful of toasted almonds. Dust with chaat masala.

Garam Masala means hot spice mix. It's a flavorful blend of cinnamon, pepper, fennel, cloves, cardamom, cumin, and more, so you get the combined cholesterol-lowering, anti-inflammatory, and immune-boosting benefits of each of the ingredients.

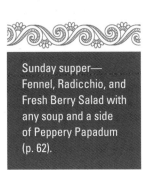
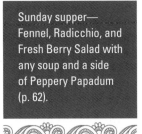

Sunday supper— Fennel, Radicchio, and Fresh Berry Salad with any soup and a side of Peppery Papadum (p. 62).

Sweet and Spicy Mango Salad

My grandfather, *Pappa*, had a long, long stick with a machete and a small net fastened to the end. We'd march out into the middle of his mango orchard and he'd lean down to ask, "Which one?" I was three or four years old, and I'd point to the very top of the trees. *Pappa* would cut the exact one, and I'd watch it drop into the bag. "For you, Deepa *mol*." A piece of the sun.

SERVES 4

Lemon-honey dressing:
2 tablespoons fresh lemon juice
1 teaspoon wild honey
½ teaspoon cayenne powder
¼ teaspoon salt

3 ripe mangoes, skin removed and sliced into long ½-inch strips
½ sweet onion, sliced as thinly as you can

Crowning flavor:
1 teaspoon chaat masala
Edible flower petals (optional)

1. Whisk lemon-honey dressing together in a glass bowl. Set aside.

2. In a large salad bowl, gently toss mango strips and onion slices with lemon-honey dressing. Serve right away. Mango salad will keep in the fridge for an hour, if you need to prep ahead.

Crowning flavor: Dust the salad with chaat masala and garnish with edible flower petals for a colorful topping.

Pairs beautifully with any of my grain and meat recipes, like Gingered Farro with Dried Fruit and Nuts (p. 64) and Tomji's Spicy Kerala Beef with Coconut Chips (p. 184). Plenty other options to pick from!

DEEPA'S SECRET
To peel a mango, take a sharp knife and slice all the way through on either side of the seed. Slice or cube (crisscross) the fruit in the peel, without piercing the peel. Now invert the peel and free the slices or cubes with a knife.

Mangoes *are a gut-friendly fruit, both high-fiber and low-glycemic for a tropical fruit. They are also high in antioxidants and vitamins, which boost immunities.*

Avocado, Tomato, and Plum Salad

My mother used to say, "Intelligence is the capacity to adapt to the unexpected." (She still managed a frown at my bad report cards.) That's the plum in this dish—I'd never had one until I came to this country. The unexpected ingredient wakes up the palate in this smart little salad.

SERVES 4

Dressing:
½ teaspoon Ginger Garlic Paste (p. 38)
½ yellow onion, minced
1 tablespoon fresh lime juice
½ teaspoon wild honey
1 jalapeno, minced
1 tablespoon extra virgin olive oil
½ teaspoon cumin seeds, toasted and
    ground
1 teaspoon salt
½ teaspoon fresh ground black pepper

2 avocados, sliced
1 large tomato, sliced
1 plum, sliced

Crowning flavor:
2 tablespoons cilantro, stemmed and
    finely chopped
4 mint leaves, roughly torn
1 teaspoon chaat masala
1 cup Go Nuts! (p. 44) or toasted
    crumbled walnuts

1. Whisk dressing ingredients together in a glass bowl. Check seasoning and set aside.

2. On a platter, mix tomato, avocado, and plum slices gently. Drizzle the dressing on top.

Crowning flavor: Sprinkle chopped cilantro, mint leaves, and chaat masala on top of the salad. I sometimes sprinkle with Go Nuts! or a handful of toasted crumbled walnuts.

Serve this salad with General Joseph's Five-Star Chicken Batons (p. 176), Lucky, Lively Black-Eyed Peas (p. 148) and/or Cauliflower and Beans Tumble (p. 138).

Wild honey: Ancient Egyptians first braved the bees to extract honey from their hives for its nutritional and medicinal properties. The antioxidants in honey boost brain health and memory. It is also a natural anti-inflammatory and cough-suppressant. Honey is a healthier replacement for sugar in a diabetic diet.

Summer Tomato Salad

In New Delhi, tomatoes never went out of season. We had one kind, the size of my five-year-old fist, which ripened on the vine year-round. I am still smitten with the variety we can get in California.

SERVES 4

Balsamic vinegar mixture:
½ cup balsamic vinegar
1 teaspoon brown sugar
¼ teaspoon cayenne powder
½ teaspoon cumin seeds, toasted and
    ground

6 medium-sized fresh vine-ripened
    yellow and red tomatoes
1 medium sweet onion, finely sliced and
    rinsed in water
1 teaspoon salt
½ teaspoon fresh ground black pepper

Crowning flavor:
6 basil leaves, torn into pieces
2 tablespoons Go Nuts! (p. 44) or
    favorite toasted seeds
½ teaspoon chaat masala
¼ cup extra virgin olive oil

1. In a shallow saucepan over medium heat, reduce balsamic vinegar mixture by half (about 3 minutes). Remove from heat and cool.

2. Cut tomatoes into thick ½-inch slices. Slice onion as finely as you can and rinse in cold water. Pat dry. Season tomatoes and onion with salt.

3. Loosely arrange tomato slices with rings of onion slices tucked underneath on a flat platter.

4. Grind pepper directly onto the tomato and onion. Drizzle with balsamic vinegar reduction.

Crowning flavor: Top with basil leaves, Go Nuts! (or favorite toasted seeds) and chaat masala. Drizzle with olive oil.

DEEPA'S SECRET
Use kitchen shears (or anoint a pair of sharp scissors) to snip, instead of chopping herbs, veggies, etc.

Summer Tomato Salad with Rotisserie chicken with Mughlai Sauce (p. 32) and Smashed Chickpea and Toasted Peanut Cakes (p. 136). Invite me over!

Kala Chola Salad

Kala Chola is Hindi for black beans, although you don't find them in many traditional Indian dishes. This is my Southeast Asian take on your Southwestern salad.

SERVES 2

Dressing:
2 tablespoons extra virgin olive oil or truffle oil
1 tablespoon white or red wine vinegar
1 tablespoon fresh lemon juice
1 teaspoon cumin seeds, toasted and ground
¼ teaspoon grated nutmeg
½ onion, finely chopped
1 garlic clove, minced
1 jalapeño, finely chopped
1 teaspoon Dijon mustard
1 teaspoon salt
½ teaspoon fresh ground black pepper

1 cup parsley, stemmed and finely chopped

1 can black beans (15 oz), drained and rinsed well

4 cups baby spinach
1 apple, thinly sliced
1 plum, thinly sliced
1 small red onion, thinly sliced, and rinsed in cold water

Crowning flavor:
Go Nuts! (p. 44)
Zest of 1 lemon

1. Whisk ingredients for dressing together in a large salad bowl. Stir in chopped parsley. Set aside.

2. Add beans. Check seasoning. Let stand for 10 minutes.

3. Toss spinach, apple, plum, and red onion slices with the beans.

Crowning flavor: Top with Go Nuts! and lemon zest.

DEEPA'S SECRET
Rinsing onion slices in water reduces their pungency so they won't overwhelm your salad or your palate.

Kala Chola Salad with A Tangle of Crab Legs in Savory Coconut Cream (p. 170), and Dryfoossels Sprouts (p. 144).

Ginger Cabbage Slaw

Picnics were the highlights of my parents' weekends. We'd pack up hard-boiled eggs, cucumber and tomato sandwiches, Ginger Cabbage Slaw, and blankets, and drive a couple of hours to sit in the shade of the orange-flowered flame tree. As kids, the drive seemed interminable. As adults, we discovered that our favorite picnic spot was exactly six miles away. My dad's Hindustan Minor clocked 10 mph on those old back roads.

SERVES 4

Dressing:
3 tablespoons toasted sesame oil
2 tablespoons fresh lemon juice
1 tablespoon sweet pickle relish
1 tablespoon Dijon mustard
1 tablespoon mayonnaise
1 tablespoon white or red wine vinegar
1 teaspoon cayenne powder
1 tablespoon kalonji (onion seeds) or
   sesame seeds
2 cups parsley, finely chopped
1 teaspoon salt
¼ teaspoon fresh ground black pepper

Salad:
½ cabbage, finely sliced (approximately
   4 cups)
1 carrot, grated
1 tablespoon Ginger Garlic Paste (p. 38)

1. Whisk dressing ingredients together in a large salad bowl.

2. Toss sliced cabbage and grated carrot with Ginger Garlic Paste and then the dressing. Check seasoning. Let stand at room temperature for 30 minutes before serving (with some toasted nuts, if you like).

Ginger *has been used to calm nausea for thousands of years in the East, and it has been proven effective by scientists in the West within the last few decades. The gingerol in ginger also has strong anti-inflammatory, antioxidant, and antiviral properties.*

Serve Ginger Cabbage Slaw with Aromatic Fish in Parchment (p. 166) and Gingered Farro with Dried Fruit and Nuts (p. 64).

Chukku's Yogurt Salad

I'd forgotten all about Chukku's yogurt until she came to visit last year. Delicious! "This must be in my cookbook! Can I?" I asked. "Of course!" she said. We've been sharing since childhood.

SERVES 4

1 baby eggplant, slivered and cut into 1-inch "confetti" strips
½ teaspoon salt (to "sweat" the eggplant)

Seasoned yogurt:
3 cups Greek yogurt
1 teaspoon salt
1 tablespoon cumin seeds, toasted and ground
1 tablespoon wild honey

2 tablespoons unrefined coconut oil

***Tadka* (fried topping):**
1 tablespoon extra virgin olive oil
1 teaspoon black mustard seeds
1 teaspoon cumin seeds
2 whole dried red chilies
1 shallot, minced
10 fresh curry leaves
2 tablespoons fresh ginger, thinly slivered
1 teaspoon black peppercorns

1 cup cucumber, slivered and cut into confetti strips

Crowning flavor:
¼ teaspoon cayenne powder
¼ teaspoon smoked paprika
1 tablespoon chopped cilantro

Make ahead: The yogurt base will keep overnight in the fridge. Fry the eggplant confetti and the *tadka* (fried topping), refrigerate separately, and reheat when ready to serve.

1. Arrange eggplant confetti in a single layer on a plate lined with paper towels. Sprinkle with salt and leave for 20 minutes. Salt helps to "sweat" the eggplant of excess moisture. Pat dry the eggplant with paper towels.

2. Whisk yogurt, salt, cumin, and wild honey in a glass bowl. Check seasoning and set aside the seasoned yogurt.

3. In a nonstick skillet, heat the unrefined coconut oil and add pat-dried eggplant confetti. Brown eggplant for about 3 minutes, stirring over medium heat. Set aside.

4. *Tadka:* In a skillet, heat the olive oil. When shimmering, add mustard seeds, cumin seeds, and whole dried red chilies. Lower heat and add minced shallot, curry leaves, ginger, and black peppercorns. Stir for 30 seconds or until fragrant. Remove from heat.

5. Top seasoned yogurt with the *tadka,* browned eggplant, and cucumber confetti (the cucumber will get enough salt from the seasoned yogurt and browned eggplant).

Crowning flavor: Sprinkle the yogurt with cayenne and paprika to create a speckled red accent against the white of the yogurt and the brown of the eggplant. Shower with chopped cilantro and serve.

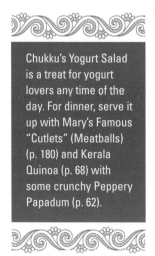

Chukku's Yogurt Salad is a treat for yogurt lovers any time of the day. For dinner, serve it up with Mary's Famous "Cutlets" (Meatballs) (p. 180) and Kerala Quinoa (p. 68) with some crunchy Peppery Papadum (p. 62).

Yogurt is a popular probiotic food. The most current science has determined that the billions of bacteria in a serving are not enough to change the actual makeup of our microbiota (our gut has tens of trillions), but it changes the way they act. Yogurt improves our bacteria's ability to digest complex carbohydrates. It will also give the immune system a boost, and the calcium and vitamin D in yogurt helps prevent bone loss.

> *"To paraphrase Arnold Edinborough:
> curiosity is the basis of education.
> If you tell me that 'curiosity killed
> the cat,' I say that cat died nobly."*
>
> —My father-in-law, A. M. Thomas (*Appachen*)

9

Savory Vegetables

Savory Vegetables

efore you go graphing my family tree, let me point out that Thomas is a common family name in Kerala. Thampy's father and my mother were not related (for as far back as we can go)—our marriage formed the union between the two Thomas branches.

A. M. Thomas grew up in Kerala, the rice bowl of India. He was the son of a paddy farmer who worked the land without the help of hired hands. He was often up before the sun, tilling until it was time to set out to school. *Appachen* (Malayalam for *father*) was the first in his family to graduate high school and go on to college. Then, after college, he wanted to go to law school. "Law school?!" *Appachen* loved to tell the story. It was the early 1940s and his grandmother didn't know what this law school was. All she needed to know was that her grandson was compelled to go. She hawked her jewelry and saw to it that he went.

After he practiced law, A. M. Thomas was elected to serve in the first parliament of independent India. He served the first three prime ministers of India before being tapped to become High Commissioner to Australia and then Zambia. As the first Christian minister (the rest of Nehru's cabinet ministers were Hindu or Muslim), *Appachen* was asked to escort Emperor Haile Selassie of Ethiopia when he visited India in 1956. Thampy inherited the Emperor's thank you gift, a set of centuries-old gold coin cufflinks.

I came into the family years later. My clearest memory? Not the Emperor, no. Dignitaries, yes. I can remember the head of the Orthodox Church waiting in the living room while I most vividly recall *Appachen* rolling up his shirt to give himself his daily insulin shot. This is a memory that came barreling back as I watched Thampy guide the needle into his belly the first handful of times.

A. M. Thomas, August 1989

A. M. Thomas swearing in at the cabinet of Prime Minister Nehru

Emperor Haile Selassie's
"thank you" gift to A. M. Thomas.

Five out of my husband's nine siblings have diabetes. I am relieved his mother, the world's best cook, never learned that the staple of her family table, *and* her husband's family's economic lifeblood, would eventually make them sick. (She herself died of complications from diabetes.)

Getting a rice bowl baby to quit his rice meant coming up with super-savory alternatives. I know Thampy is not the only one with a thing for rice, and then there are all the potato-heads—I get it, it's comfort food. It's just that your gut doesn't get it. Potatoes actually top rice on the glycemic index. Both will produce that glucose spike you want to avoid.

Within a few weeks, Thampy was off of rice (and then off of insulin) and onto heritage barley—same steamy mouthfeel, but full of nutrients and fiber. I'll point potato-people toward cauliflower—roasted, grilled, or mashed—your preference. Even if you're not genetically predisposed to diabetes, high blood pressure, or heart disease, some of the latest research on aging also links dementia with high carb consumption.

Here are fifteen of my favorite veggie concoctions that are anything but bland. Serve them up as sides or in emperor-sized portions for mains. Pledge a healthy allegiance . . .

Aviel

Aviel is Malayalam for vegetable medley. It is the celebration dish in Kerala. I kept the concept, but I didn't feel the need to cook it to a mush-like consistency. This vegetable medley is al dente—a lot faster, a lot fresher, and every bit as festive.

SERVES 4

Yogurt dressing:
2 cups grated coconut (thawed if frozen)
1 cup water
1 tablespoon cumin seeds, toasted and ground
1 jalapeño, rough chopped
1 tablespoon fresh ginger paste
½ teaspoon fresh garlic paste
1 cup Greek yogurt

Vegetables (cut into 2-inch sticks resembling French fries):
2 Yukon gold potatoes, peeled
2 cups string beans
1 carrot
1 zucchini
1 yellow, red, and orange bell pepper (3 in all)

Sauté:
1 tablespoon unrefined coconut oil
1 yellow onion (cut into 2-inch pieces resembling French fries)
6 curry leaves
½ teaspoon salt
½ teaspoon fresh ground black pepper

Tadka:
1 tablespoon unrefined coconut oil
1 teaspoon black mustard seeds
6 curry leaves
1 shallot, sliced
¼ teaspoon cayenne flakes

1 tablespoon unrefined coconut oil (melted over low heat) for finishing drizzle

1. Puree yogurt dressing ingredients in a blender or food processor. Set aside.

2. Vegetables: Blanch potatoes and beans in a large pot of salted boiling water for 2 minutes. Add carrots, blanch for 1 minute more. Add zucchini and bell peppers, blanch for 1 additional minute. Vegetables should be firmly cooked, not mushy! Drain.

3. Heat coconut oil and sauté onion. When onion begins to brown, add curry leaves (protect yourself from crackling leaves, with a lid) and stir for 30 seconds. Add blanched vegetables and continue sautéing for 2 minutes. Don't overcook! Season with salt and pepper.

4. Add yogurt dressing to the sautéed vegetables and toss gently to avoid breaking up the vegetables.

5. *Tadka:* Heat coconut oil in a large 12-inch saucepan over medium heat. Add mustard seeds and curry leaves (shield yourself from spluttering with a lid). Add shallot and stir until it begins to brown (5 minutes). Lower heat, and add cayenne flakes. Stir for one minute, and spoon *tadka* over the sautéed and yogurt-dressed vegetables.

6. Drizzle with a final tablespoon of coconut oil as a flavor booster! Check seasoning. Serve warm or at room temperature.

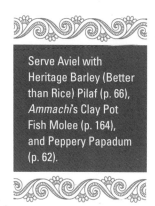

Serve Aviel with Heritage Barley (Better than Rice) Pilaf (p. 66), *Ammachi*'s Clay Pot Fish Molee (p. 164), and Peppery Papadum (p. 62).

*The humble **onion** promotes the growth of healthy gut bacteria, which is good for digestion, immune response, and brain function. The inulin in onion also stabilizes blood sugar levels, helping to control diabetes. Onions contain powerful antioxidants, and red and purple onions have anthocyanins (the same water-soluble pigments found in berries) with powerful anti-inflammatory and antimicrobial properties.*

Best-Ever Oven-Roasted Swee' Potato Fries

French fries weren't a fast food when I was growing up. We loved our "crisps"—potato chips with ketchup. Happy note to self: What used to be a craving is now just a memory . . . My version of oven-baked fries, I hope, is deeply satisfying and guilt-free!

SERVES 6

2 sweet potatoes, cut into evenly sized
   fry-wedges (skin on is fine)
2 shallots, sliced
1 teaspoon cayenne flakes
1 tablespoon fennel seeds
2 tablespoons extra virgin olive oil
1½ teaspoons salt

Crowning flavor:
½ teaspoon chaat masala

Make ahead: Bake the fries (15–20 minutes) up to a day ahead and store in a single layer on a baking sheet in the fridge. Finish roasting (15–20 minutes) just before serving. Twice-baked fries are even crisper!

1. Heat oven to 400°F.

2. Mix and toss all ingredients (except chaat masala) on a baking sheet lined with parchment paper and roast for 30–40 minutes. Stir and rotate once, halfway through. Check more frequently towards the end of the baking time to make sure they don't burn. Reheat before serving to crisp up!

Crowning flavor: Finish with chaat masala. Check seasoning and serve warm!

Serve Best-Ever Oven-Roasted Swee' Potato Fries, Chop Chop Lamb Chops (p. 182), and Summer Tomato Salad (p. 118).

Fennel seed is a potent antioxidant and anti-inflammatory which can help manage heart disease, type 2 diabetes, and arthritis. The taste is similar to anise, but anise and fennel are two different plants in the same botanical family. The fennel plant can be eaten in its entirety. Lucknow fennel, an intense small-seed variety, is prized for its particular sweetness and aroma.

Quick Chana Masala

Quick! *Phatta phat!* There were times I thought *phatta phat* was my middle name—walking, doing homework, and, yes, eating! As soon as I was served my plate, I was being told to hurry—*phatta phat*! *Deepa, please, I'd like to clear the table!* You can cook my chana masala in a hurry, but you don't have to.

SERVES 6

3 tablespoons grapeseed oil
1 teaspoon (Lucknow) fennel seeds
2-inch cinnamon stick
2 black cardamom pods
½ onion, finely chopped

2 garlic cloves, ground to a paste in a
    food processor
½-inch piece fresh ginger, skinned and
    ground to a paste
4 teaspoons Deepa's Secret Spice
    (p. 24) (or ⅓ teaspoon each garam
    masala, ground cumin, and allspice)

½ teaspoon turmeric
¼ cup water
3 cans (15 oz each) garbanzo beans,
    drained and rinsed well
2 tablespoons ketchup or Chutput
    Ketchup (p. 36)
1 teaspoon salt

Crowning flavor:
2 tablespoons Reemsie's Tamarind
    Sauce (p. 34)
1 tablespoon chaat masala
½ cup New Indian Gremolata (p. 60) or
    chopped onion, rinsed in cold water
    and strained

1. Heat oil in a wok or a deep 10-inch saucepan.

2. Add fennel seeds, cinnamon, and cardamom, and cook for one minute. Add onion and cook until light brown (about three minutes).

3. Add ginger and garlic pastes, Deepa's Secret Spice, turmeric, and water. Stir well.

4. Add garbanzo beans, Chutput Ketchup, and salt. Cover and cook for 10 minutes, stirring occasionally. Remove from heat.

Crowning flavor: Mix in Reemsie's Tamarind Sauce. Sprinkle chaat masala and New Indian Gremolata or rinsed chopped onions. Check seasoning.

DEEPA'S SECRET

Chana Masala (not to be confused with chana dal, which is the split kernel of a variety of garbanzo, also called Bengal Gram) is a moniker for Indian street food, and Indian street food is all about the layers. In this case, tamarind sauce, gremolata, chopped onion—or you could try a drizzle of Greek yogurt, seasoned with salt and pepper. Trust me, you can't go wrong!

Serve with Oatmeal Uppma (p. 70), Dal for Dummies! (p. 56) and Tousled Haricots Verts and Caramelized Carrots (p. 154).

Smashed Chickpea and Toasted Peanut Cakes

Vendors in Delhi used to toast peanuts on the streets during the cooler winter months. They'd light fires and warm the peanuts in their shells, then slip them into newspaper cones. The peanut-chickpea combo doubles the protein in this recipe for a great vegetarian meal, side, snack, or appetizer.

SERVES 6

Toast and grind:
¼ teaspoon anise seeds
¼ teaspoon cumin seeds
¼ teaspoon coriander seeds
¼ teaspoon fennel seeds

1 can (15 oz) garbanzo beans, drained and rinsed well
1 cup peanuts, shelled, toasted, and rough chopped (skin-on Indian peanuts are fine)
1 cup unsweetened shredded coconut
2 tablespoons onion, minced
2 tablespoons garlic, minced
1 jalapeño, minced
½ teaspoon garam masala
1 teaspoon chaat masala
¼ teaspoon cayenne powder
1 tablespoon mint leaves, stemmed and finely chopped
1 tablespoon cilantro leaves, stemmed and finely chopped
1 egg, beaten
1 teaspoon fresh lemon juice
½ teaspoon salt

1 cup coconut or chickpea (garbanzo) flour
1 tablespoon unrefined coconut oil

Make ahead: Cakes, cooked or uncooked, freeze beautifully for a grab and go snack, appetizer, or meal. Use parchment or waxed paper to separate layers before freezing.

1. Toast and grind seeds. Mix all the remaining ingredients except for the flour and coconut oil. Use a hand blender to puree to a rough consistency. Check seasoning.

2. Shape into 2-inch patties.

3. Press patties into coconut or chickpea flour to help them hold their shape.

4. Heat oil in a 10-inch nonstick skillet. Use enough oil to "moisten" the pan (about one tablespoon).

5. Brown the cakes (several at a time, without crowding) over medium heat (about four minutes). Gently flip (I use two spatulas) and brown the other side (another four minutes). Repeat until all cakes are done. You may need to add oil between batches. Keep the finished cakes warm in a 200°F oven until ready to serve.

6. Serve with Reemsie's Tamarind Sauce (p. 34) or Chutput Ketchup (p. 36) for dipping.

The chickpea and peanut cakes are a nice starter or accompaniment to Crackling Okra (p. 140) and Chukku's Yogurt Salad (p. 124).

Cauliflower and Beans Tumble

Cauliflower, or *gobi*, is commonly paired with potatoes and peas in the dish *aloo matar gobi*. This uncommon pairing has fewer carbs and more protein. It's my experience that uncommon pairings—*Amma* and *Dada*, Thampy and me—can bring out the best in each ingredient.

SERVES 6

1 large whole cauliflower, sliced into
 ½-inch florets

Seeds and dried spices:
1 teaspoon cumin seeds
1 teaspoon mustard seeds
1 teaspoon (Lucknow) fennel seeds
¼ teaspoon grated nutmeg
¼ teaspoon cayenne flakes
½ teaspoon turmeric
1 teaspoon salt
¼ teaspoon fresh ground black pepper

2 tablespoons unrefined coconut oil,
 melted over low heat (divided)

½ cup shallots, finely chopped
¼ cup shredded coconut (unsweetened)
2 tablespoons Ginger Garlic Paste
 (p. 38)
1 jalapeño, quartered lengthwise with
 top intact
10 curry leaves

4 cups Italian beans, sliced (on a
 diagonal) into ¼-inch pieces

Crowning flavor:
Zest of 1 lemon
2 tablespoons fresh lemon juice
1 tablespoon Magic Finishing Spice
 (p. 28) or chaat masala

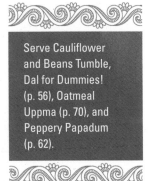

Serve Cauliflower
and Beans Tumble,
Dal for Dummies!
(p. 56), Oatmeal
Uppma (p. 70), and
Peppery Papadum
(p. 62).

1. Preheat oven to 450°F. Place cauliflower in a single layer on a parchment-lined baking tray. Sprinkle with half the seeds and dried spices. Drizzle with one tablespoon coconut oil. Roast for 15 minutes, or to preferred doneness.

2. Heat one tablespoon of coconut oil in a deep 10-inch saucepan over medium heat. When shimmering, add remaining seeds and dried spices. As seeds begin to pop, add shallots and stir until light brown (two minutes). Add shredded coconut, Ginger Garlic Paste, jalapeño, and curry leaves. Add beans, stir well, cover, and cook for 3 minutes. Check for doneness.

3. Fold in cauliflower with the beans. Check seasoning.

Crowning flavor: Top the cauliflower beans tumble with lemon zest and juice. A sprinkle of my Magic Finishing Spice or chaat masala will add more flavor notes.

Turmeric is in almost every Indian dish, and the incidence of chronic disease (except diabetes) among Indians is lower than in the West. (Turmeric-treated Band-Aids are popular in India.) Naturally, scientists have looked for a correlation. The curcumin in turmeric has been linked to health benefits. It aids diabetes control and supports heart health. Benefits of turmeric are still being widely studied.

Crackling Okra

If you like okra, you'll love this recipe. If you don't like okra, it's because you haven't tasted crispy okra. This is not your goopy gumbo variety. Okra is one of India's most popular vegetables.

SERVES 4

3 tablespoons unrefined coconut oil

3 cups fresh okra, sliced into ¼-inch pieces

1 teaspoon mustard seeds

1 teaspoon split urad dal

1 jalapeño, slit with top intact

1 shallot, finely chopped

Shredded coconut mix (blended in a food processor to a rough consistency):

3 cloves garlic

¼ teaspoon cayenne flakes

1 cup shredded coconut

¼ teaspoon turmeric

¼ teaspoon asafoetida

1 teaspoon red or white vinegar

4 curry leaves

1 teaspoon salt

½ teaspoon fresh ground black pepper

1 tablespoon fresh lemon juice

1. Heat oil to shimmering in a 10-inch nonstick skillet over medium-high heat.

2. Add mustard seeds and urad dal (shielding yourself with a lid to protect from spluttering). When the urad dal begins to brown, add jalapeño. After 1 minute, add shallot and stir for 2 minutes.

3. Add shredded coconut mix. Sauté for 2 minutes, stirring to avoid burning. Add sliced okra and sauté at high heat, without burning, for 2 minutes. Give okra plenty of room to crisp up. Taste to check seasoning and crispness. Don't overcook! Remove from heat. A squeeze of lemon on top will perk up the flavor.

Okra: *Roasted okra seeds have been used to treat diabetes in Turkey for years. The added benefits of the high fiber and antioxidant properties make okra a vegetable worth eating again, and again.*

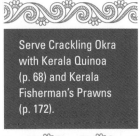

Serve Crackling Okra with Kerala Quinoa (p. 68) and Kerala Fisherman's Prawns (p. 172).

Ralph's Garlicky Spinach a la Dal

SERVES 6

2 cups chana dal, rinsed well
   and drained

Dal base:
1-inch piece fresh ginger,
   minced
8 fresh curry leaves
1 teaspoon cayenne flakes
1 teaspoon turmeric
2 cloves
1 cardamom pod
¼ teaspoon cinnamon
1 tablespoon red or white
   vinegar
1 teaspoon salt

Dal topping:
5 mint leaves, stemmed and
   rough chopped
¼ cup cilantro, stemmed and
   rough chopped
1 jalapeño, seeded and finely
   chopped
1 shallot, finely chopped
1 tablespoon unrefined coconut
   oil (melted over low heat)

Spinach:
1 tablespoon extra virgin olive
   oil
1 teaspoon cumin seeds
2 shallots, sliced
½ teaspoon cayenne flakes
10 garlic cloves, minced
¼ teaspoon grated nutmeg
2 cups fresh parsley leaves,
   chopped
6 cups baby spinach (¾ lb)
1 tablespoon balsamic vinegar
½ teaspoon salt
¼ teaspoon fresh ground black
   pepper

Crowning flavor:
½ cup New Indian Gremolata
   (p. 60)
½ cup Caramelized Shallots
   (p. 58) (optional)
½ teaspoon chaat masala

Ralph Oswald

Thampy and I met restaurateur Ralph Oswald when we were getting ready to sell our first house. Ralph and his wife Barbara owned a beautiful house Ralph had built by hand on part of the former Folgers' Estate in Woodside. I fell in love with the place; but Thampy and I would've been laughed out of the bank in our start-up days. Ralph looked at me and said, "Deepa, you are going to raise your sons here." And that was it. He took stock in Deepa Textiles as part of our down payment; and I am not kidding when I say that over the next ten years, I worked my cheeks off, in good part to pay Ralph back.

Years after the last of the restaurants were sold—Ralph was in his eighties—you would still find him in his kitchen. He insisted food was "the great leveler." There would be a veritable U.N. around the table, and Ralph would preside from the counter, those tireless, generous hands chopping away. This recipe, an international meet-up, is my small tribute to a man to whom I owe so much.

Make ahead: The dal can be made ahead and kept in the fridge or frozen.

1. Dal preparation: Put rinsed dal in a heavy saucepan. Add the base ingredients and just enough water to cover dal. Cover partially and cook, stirring occasionally until dal is tender, but still has a bite to it (about 20 minutes). Add water if needed while cooking; you can drain off any excess water when dal is finished cooking.

2. Check seasoning. Mix mint leaves with cilantro, seeded jalapeño, and shallot. Gently stir in topping without smashing the dal. Drizzle with coconut oil.

3. Spinach preparation: Heat olive oil in a 10-inch saucepan over medium heat. Add cumin seeds and cook for one minute. Add shallots and brown lightly. Add cayenne flakes, garlic, and nutmeg. Stir for 30 seconds, careful not to burn the garlic. Add parsley and stir for one minute. Then add spinach and cook until wilted (30 seconds) or leave raw, if you prefer a salad presentation. Remove from heat. Stir in balsamic vinegar, salt, and pepper.

4. Arrange chana dal in the center of a platter with spinach around it.

Crowning flavor: For added finish, top with New Indian Gremolata and Caramelized Shallots (optional), and sprinkle chaat masala over the entire dish.

"*Whenever Barbara and I fought, we chose a recipe and cooked it together.*"
—Ralph Oswald, Bay Area restaurateur and founder of the Village Pub (Woodside's only Michelin star restaurant)

DEEPA'S SECRET
Leave a wooden spoon in the pot to
prevent dal from bubbling over.

Ralph's Spinach a
la Dal complements
Ammachi's Clay pot
Fish Molee (p. 164) or
Nawabi Tuna Kebab
Burger (p. 174).

Dryfoossels Sprouts

Two things about Susan Dryfoos: She loves Brussels sprouts, and she hates to cook. This is easily the most popular Thanksgiving vegetable on our table. This is a small culinary salute to my great friend and all she's done for me (see Chapter 14).

SERVES 4

Dressing: (whisked together)
2 tablespoons unrefined coconut oil
   (melted over low heat)
¼ teaspoon cinnamon
¼ teaspoon grated nutmeg
¼ teaspoon turmeric
½ teaspoon cayenne powder
¼ teaspoon allspice
1 tablespoon pure maple syrup
1 teaspoon salt
1 teaspoon fresh ground black pepper
1 teaspoon balsamic vinegar

1 lb Brussels sprouts, trimmed and
   halved
3 tablespoons dried cranberries
   (unsweetened)
¼ cup apple juice or water

Crowning flavor:
¼ cup unsalted macadamia nuts,
   toasted and rough chopped
1 teaspoon chaat masala

1. Preheat oven to 425°F. Line a baking tray with parchment paper.

2. Prepare dressing in a large glass bowl.

3. Mix Brussels sprouts with the dressing. Roast in a single layer for fifteen minutes, stirring and rotating the tray once.

4. In the meantime, in a small covered saucepan, gently heat cranberries in apple juice until liquid is absorbed and cranberries are plumped (about 6 minutes).

5. Mix cranberries with roasting Brussels sprouts and return to oven until Brussels sprouts are tender but not mushy and a few leaves begin to brown (about five minutes). You could give it a quick broil to singe some of the sprout leaves lightly (about one minute, don't burn!).

Crowning flavor: Top with macadamia nuts and chaat masala.

Brussels sprouts have a surprising amount of nutrients for their size. A cupful delivers more than the recommended daily allowance of vitamins C and K. And, like other cruciferous vegetables, they can help prevent disease, obesity, diabetes, and brain dysfunction. A lot of good things in a very small package.

Dryfoossel's Sprouts (a great addition for Thanksgiving dinner), Keema Spicy Beef (p. 186), and Sweet and Spicy Mango Salad (p. 114).

Eggplant Roulades

I suppose I could have called them eggplant roll-ups. My mother was a wonderful hostess. Her secret: Honor and nurture the guests. It's too easy (and stressful) to get caught up trying to impress. These roulades look and taste impressive, but they're simple enough to make.

SERVES 4

2 eggplants
1 tablespoon salt
1 tablespoon extra virgin olive oil
1 tablespoon cumin seeds, toasted and ground
1 teaspoon sriracha, or to taste
1 tablespoon store-bought pesto
2 cups Parmesan cheese, grated (divided)
2 (12 oz) jars roasted red bell peppers, Italian style (in water)—I like Italbrand
1 tablespoon mint leaves, stemmed and finely chopped
1 tablespoon cilantro leaves, stemmed and finely chopped

Crowning flavor:
1 cup New Indian Gremolata (p. 60)
1 tablespoon chaat masala

Start with Tomato Rasam (p. 92) as a soup. Then serve Eggplant Roulades with Aromatic Fish in Parchment (p. 166).

1. Position rack in the middle of the oven and preheat oven to 400°F. Line a baking tray with parchment paper and set aside. You will also need two additional trays lined with paper towels for the process.

2. Slice eggplants lengthwise (¼-inch thick). Discard the two end pieces with the skin.

3. Place eggplant slices in a single layer on one of the trays lined with paper towels. Sprinkle the slices with salt to release excess moisture. You can stack the slices as long as you place paper towels between your layers to absorb the moisture. Set aside for 20 minutes and then pat each slice dry with more paper towels.

4. Heat 1 tablespoon of olive oil in a 12-inch nonstick skillet. Lightly brown eggplant slices on both sides, 1–2 minutes per side. Return browned slices to the second tray lined with paper towels. Continue until all eggplant slices are browned (adding oil to the skillet as needed).

5. Place browned eggplant slices, individually, on the remaining parchment-lined baking tray. Dust eggplant with ground cumin seeds. Brush with sriracha and pesto. (Go light on the siracha if you want less heat.) Sprinkle with Parmesan cheese. (Reserve a cup of cheese for garnish.)

6. Pat roasted bell peppers dry with paper towels and place a single piece on each eggplant slice. Sprinkle lightly again with Parmesan cheese, and with chopped mint and cilantro leaves. Tightly roll each stack of eggplant and bell pepper. Arrange rolls, open end down, on the parchment-lined baking tray. (Don't crowd.)

7. Sprinkle rolls with remaining cheese. Bake for 15 minutes or until cheese browns.

Crowning flavor: Top with New Indian Gremolata and a few dashes of chaat masala for extra flavor. Serve hot!

Lucky, Lively Black-Eyed Peas

Indians are among the most superstitious people on the planet. In India, moving house on a Saturday is bad luck. Wedding dates are set by the position of the moon and stars, and I've thrown mountains of salt over my left shoulder, which has, knock on wood, delivered this long, healthy life. However, I'd never heard of eating black-eyed peas for good luck on New Year's. It's a part of Jewish and Southern traditions.

SERVES 6

3 cups black-eyed peas, dried (soaked overnight, or 6 cups canned black-eyed peas)

Spice mix:
½ teaspoon turmeric
½ teaspoon allspice
½ teaspoon cayenne powder
3 black cardamom pods
12 curry leaves
1 jalapeño, slit with top intact
4 garlic cloves, smashed
1-inch cinnamon stick

1½ teaspoon salt

Tadka (fried topping):
2 tablespoons unrefined coconut oil
1 teaspoon cumin seeds
1 onion, finely chopped
6 curry leaves
¼ teaspoon cayenne flakes
½ teaspoon salt

1 tablespoon fresh lemon juice

Crowning flavor:
2 cups New Indian Gremolata (p. 60)

Make ahead: If you're using dried peas, they'll need to soak overnight. You can make and refrigerate or freeze the cooked black-eyed peas ahead of time, then prepare the *tadka* just before serving.

1. For dried peas: If you are using dried peas soaked overnight, rinse and drain well. Put peas in deep pot with enough water just to cover. Add the spice mix and simmer until tender but not mushy (about 15 minutes). Remove from heat. Drain off any excess water, and season with salt.

2. For canned peas: If you are using canned peas, rinse well and drain. Add the spice mix to the black-eyed peas in a deep pot and toss gently on medium heat for 10 minutes. Remove from heat.

3. *Tadka:* Heat coconut oil in an 8-inch skillet over medium-high heat until oil starts shimmering (about a couple of minutes). Add cumin seeds and cook until fragrant (about 30 seconds). Add onion. When onion begins to brown (about one minute), add curry leaves (protecting yourself with a lid). Once spluttering stops, add cayenne flakes and salt. Pour the *tadka* over cooked peas, and stir gently.

4. Mix in lemon juice. Check seasoning.

5. Serve warm on a deeply colored platter (the contrast of a dark platter and light-colored peas is great!).

Crowning flavor: Top with New Indian Gremolata. Leave cinnamon stick on top as a garnish.

Lucky, Lively Black-Eyed Peas round out a main of New Indian Cacciatore (p. 178) with a side of Oatmeal Uppma (p. 70).

Black-eyed peas, or more accurately, black-eyed beans, are another member of the legume family. They are high in fiber, iron, and potassium, which help regulate blood pressure. And they may bring you good luck.

Hot 'n' Crispy Cabbage

Cabbage is very popular in India. I'm pretty sure my dad invented the cabbage diet. It's the one time I can remember him in the kitchen. My mother quit on his fourth day; she refused to cut open another head, and none of us could take the smell. So, my dad up and made it for himself. Somehow cabbage survived as a family favorite. This stir-fry can be served under, over, and alongside a multitude of dishes. If you keep it crunchy, it smells just fine.

SERVES 4

2 tablespoons unrefined coconut oil
1 teaspoon brown mustard seeds
1 teaspoon black sesame seeds
1 teaspoon split urad dal
2 whole dried red chilies, crushed
1 tablespoon pine nuts
1 teaspoon asafoetida (or substitute dry mustard powder)
15 curry leaves
1 cabbage, thinly sliced (approximately 8 cups)
1 tablespoon Ginger Garlic Paste (p. 38)
1 carrot, peeled, and then run peeler down length of carrot to create "ribbons"
1 tablespoon fresh lemon juice
1 tablespoon salt
1 teaspoon fresh ground black pepper

Crowning flavor:
1 cup Spicy Snacking Peanuts (p. 46)

1. Heat oil in a deep skillet until shimmering (about a couple of minutes; don't walk away!). Add mustard seeds. Partially cover to protect yourself from popping. Add sesame seeds, urad dal, crushed whole red chilies, pine nuts, and asafoetida. Stir for 30 seconds or until pine nuts start to brown.

2. Add curry leaves, cabbage, Ginger Garlic Paste, and carrot ribbons. Toss vigorously with two ladles or tongs. Remove from heat while cabbage is still crunchy (less than ten minutes) and sprinkle with lemon juice. Add salt and pepper, and check seasoning.

Crowning flavor: Top with a handful of Spicy Snacking Peanuts.

Serve with Nawabi Tuna Kebab Burger (p. 174) and Quick Chana Masala (p. 134).

DEEPA'S SECRET

I guess it's not really a secret—my dad was onto it and there are countless cabbage soup diets, but I credit cabbage with many pounds of personal weight loss over the years. It's healthy, deliciously filling, and low calorie. Don't go cabbage soup-crazy, but you could customize your own cabbage diet and lose the weight without feeling hungry.

Asafoetida: *Foetida is Latin for stinky. Use it, don't smell it. Uncooked, asafoetida or "devil's dung" lives up to its name. However, it's also known as "food of the gods." When cooked, it imparts a smooth, leek-like flavor and it's an antiflatulent to boot. Or not to boot.*

Disappearing Leftovers: *Fry a couple of eggs and serve sunny-side up on top of a bed of leftover cabbage for breakfast, lunch, or the next day's dinner.*

Rustic Vegetable Roast

What this dish lacks in formality, it makes up for in flavor. Stir some cooked lentils into the mixture when it comes out of the oven and it makes a hearty main dish.

SERVES 6

Dressing:
3 tablespoons extra virgin olive oil
2 tablespoons balsamic vinegar
1 tablespoon fresh ginger, grated
1 garlic clove, minced
2 green onions, white part only, chopped
½ cup mint leaves, stemmed and rough chopped
½ cup cilantro, stemmed and rough chopped
1 tablespoon fresh lemon juice
1 tablespoon lemon zest
1 teaspoon salt
½ teaspoon fresh ground black pepper

Vegetables: (cut into 1-inch cubes)
2 small eggplants (I like Japanese eggplants)
2 bell peppers (red and yellow)
1 red onion
Add any other vegetables you like—whole asparagus, chopped carrot, kernels of corn, thick slices of radish, sliced mushrooms, etc.

Herbs and spices:
4 garlic cloves, smashed
1 jalapeño, minced
2 tablespoons thyme
2 tablespoons fennel seeds
½ tablespoon cayenne flakes
1 teaspoon salt

Optional:
1 cup lentils
2 cups water
1 teaspoon salt
1 tablespoon extra virgin olive oil

Make ahead: Roasted veggies (steps 1–3). Warm the roasted veggies and drizzle with dressing just before serving so that the roasted vegetables retain crispness.

1. Preheat oven to 400°F.

2. Whisk dressing in a glass bowl and set aside.

3. Mix all vegetables and all herbs and spices together on a baking sheet lined with parchment paper. Roast in a single layer for 30–40 minutes, stirring and rotating once at twenty minutes. Check for doneness. A little browning is good, but avoid burning.

4. Optional: While vegetables are roasting, cook lentils in salted water in a deep saucepan (partially covered), just until tender (about ten minutes). Drain any excess water to keep the dal from getting mushy. (This is important to the texture, taste, and the visual aesthetics.) Drizzle with olive oil.

5. Remove roasted vegetables from the oven. Drizzle with whisked dressing.

Optional: If you made dal, then mix it with the roasted vegetables now. Check seasoning and serve.

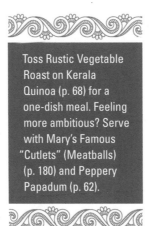

Toss Rustic Vegetable Roast on Kerala Quinoa (p. 68) for a one-dish meal. Feeling more ambitious? Serve with Mary's Famous "Cutlets" (Meatballs) (p. 180) and Peppery Papadum (p. 62).

Disappearing Leftovers: Leftover roasted vegetables are another great base for an egg breakfast the next day. Or add Rustic Vegetables (and cooked dal, if you made some) to well-seasoned broth (just enough to cover the vegetables) in a saucepan. Heat thoroughly. Top with Caramelized Shallots (p. 58) and enjoy a weekday/weeknight soup.

Tousled Haricots Verts and Caramelized Carrots

I think we had green beans eight nights a week when I was a kid! Green beans and carrots was a welcome variation. I've improved on the carrots— lightly caramelized in a little maple syrup—for my grownup do-over. It's a hit with all ages.

SERVES 4

Dressing:
1 shallot, minced
1 teaspoon Ginger Garlic Paste (p. 38)
¼ teaspoon cayenne flakes
¼ teaspoon cumin seeds, toasted and
    ground
Zest of 1 lemon
2 tablespoons fresh lemon juice
2 tablespoons toasted sesame oil
1 teaspoon salt
½ teaspoon fresh ground black pepper

1 lb haricots verts or string beans,
    trimmed

For caramelized carrots:
2 tablespoons extra virgin olive oil
1 tablespoon butter
1 bunch (8–10) carrots, trimmed and
    peeled
½ teaspoon salt
½ teaspoon fresh ground black pepper
1 teaspoon pure maple syrup

1. Whisk dressing ingredients together in a glass bowl and set aside.

2. Blanch the beans for 4 minutes in a pot of boiling salted water. Drain and plunge into ice-cold water to keep the beans crunchy. Drain when cool, toss with dressing and set aside.

3. Caramelize the carrots: Heat oil and butter in a large 12-inch skillet over medium heat. Add carrots, season with salt and pepper and toss occasionally for 4 minutes. Add maple syrup, lower heat and cook, tossing occasionally, for another 4–5 minutes.

4. Mix carrots with dressed beans, check seasoning, and serve in a colorful tumble.

Disappearing Leftovers: Heat a can of tomatoes in a pan. Season with a pinch of cayenne flakes and a pinch of ancho chili powder. Add the leftover veggies chopped into bite-size pieces, heat thoroughly, and enjoy as a vegetable stew!

I love this Tousled Haricots Verts and Caramelized Carrots with Truck Stop Pork Chop (p. 188) and Kala Chola Salad (p. 120).

Winter Squash and Pearl Onion

Thampy's mother grew squash in her backyard in New Delhi. Every summer, she'd give a few to my father, a gift from an over-endowed gardener to an ardent squash fan. Later, she sang a different tune: "You took my squash until you could take my son."

SERVES 6

3 cups squash (yellow), halved and sliced into ¼-inch crescent shapes

Roasting ingredients:
½ teaspoon cayenne flakes
½ teaspoon turmeric
¼ teaspoon fennel seeds
½ teaspoon cumin seeds
⅛ teaspoon grated nutmeg
⅛ teaspoon allspice
2 tablespoons unrefined coconut oil (melted over low heat)
1 tablespoon red wine vinegar
2 tablespoons Medjool dates, finely chopped
10 curry leaves
¾ teaspoon salt

1¼ cup water
1 teaspoon coconut oil
¼ teaspoon salt
1 cup pearl onions, fresh (peeled) or frozen
½ teaspoon fresh ground black pepper

1. Preheat oven to 400°F.

2. Toss squash with roasting ingredients and spread on a parchment paper-lined baking sheet. Roast in single layer without crowding, for 10 minutes. Stir, rotate, and roast until done (about seven minutes).

3. Place water, coconut oil, and salt in an 8-inch saucepan. Cook the pearl onions, covered, for 5 minutes. Uncover and cook, stirring occasionally, until done (not mushy!).

4. Mix the roasted squash and cooked pearl onions together and check seasoning. (Before serving, I like to broil the squash and pearl onions for a minute to get a bit of a char.) Add fresh ground pepper to taste.

Medjool dates—The "king of dates" has also been called the healthiest natural sweetener. You'll feel an energy-lift from the extra sugar. (People with diabetes can consume dates in smaller quantities, part of rather than the main ingredient of a snack or meal.)

Winter Squash and Pearl Onion, Tomji's Spicy Kerala Beef with Coconut Chips (p. 184), Heritage Barley (Better than Rice Pilaf) (p. 66), and Sucy's Lemon Pickle with Medjool Dates (p. 42).

Zucchini LaSuzy

This is a creative take on the popular Indian dish *lasooni* (meaning garlicky), which I've named after my creative friend Suzy Becker, *New York Times* best-selling author-illustrator of *All I Need to Know I Learned from My Cat*. All I need to know about writing, I learned from Suzy.

SERVES 4

Dressing:
2 garlic cloves, chopped
¼ small onion, finely chopped
¼ teaspoon allspice
½ teaspoon cayenne flakes
1 tablespoon fresh lemon or grapefruit juice
1 tablespoon sesame oil

1 tablespoon sesame seed oil
2 zucchinis, thinly sliced lengthwise by hand or with a mandolin
¼ teaspoon salt

Crowning flavor:
Zest of 1 lemon
½ teaspoon chaat masala

1. Mix dressing in a blender and set aside.

2. Heat 1 tablespoon of sesame oil in a wide nonstick skillet over medium heat. Add zucchini and turn gently for one minute. Sprinkle with salt. Please don't overcook.

3. Remove from heat and toss with dressing. Check seasoning.

Crowning flavor: Sprinkle lemon zest and chaat masala.

Serve alongside Keema Spicy Beef (p. 186) with Quick Onion Pickle (p. 40).

Cayenne: Cayenne is used in Ayurvedic medicine to treat digestive and circulatory issues, arthritis, and infection. The cayenne flakes include the seeds, which intensify the heat. The heat is believed to stimulate metabolism and support weight loss. Red peppers are also full of vitamins and antioxidants.

"*If you are happy, tell me of your life in this foreign land . . .*"

—The Kerala Fisherman

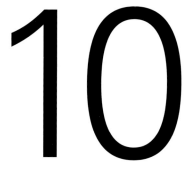

Vegetarians, don't leave me!
You can substitute tofu or bulk up the vegetables. Ammachi's Clay Pot Carrot, Beans, Cauliflower Molee. *You won't want to miss out on the flavor.*

Fish. Chicken. Meat.

Fish. Chicken. Meat.

hree years after I moved to the United States, Thampy and I went "home" for my brother Tomji's wedding. The wedding itself was in Coonoor, tea-estate country in Tamilnadu, in the southeast of India. Then, after the wedding, I flew to Kerala, to Trivandrum, where my parents had built their retirement home.

While Coonoor and Trivandrum are both about 1,500 miles away from New Delhi, where I grew up (technically what you'd call "home"), I learned in this journey that "home" is where the heart is.

Thampy didn't make the southern leg of the trip. He'd gone back to Stanford, where he was mired in work. I had taken myself to the beach at Cape Comorin, the very southernmost tip of the southernmost state, where three oceans were washing over my bare feet. (100 rupees if you can name them!*) The sun was setting, the beach glowed raspberry-orange, and my *Kurta* billowed out over my leggings.

A fisherman caught my eye, his brown skin wizened, like the rock behind him. I smiled and nodded, and was moved to share (as I often am in the face of strangers) the inner peace his waters brought me. My Malayalam (his language) failed to elicit the slightest expression, much less a verbal response, so I breezily segued into one of my wedding sound bites, again in Malayalam, about all the promise my new American life held. Again, the crags stayed frozen. I dared ask, "You are not interested in my story?"

He answered, "If you are happy, tell me of your life in this foreign land . . . if you are not, go and fix it. Then, come back and tell me of your life in this foreign land."

Happy is such a Western word, cue butterflies and unicorns. My translation doesn't do the old fisherman justice—at peace, content, or fulfilled? His simple sentences had ripped through my gauzy peace, and now with the sun below the water, I walked purposefully back to the parking lot. I *would* fix it.

Took me forty years—a lot of those years were happy—but this inner peace . . . some of it comes with

Kerala Fisherman floating dry coconut tree fronds out to the backwaters for fish to hatch their eggs in safety.

the wizening, the age after which you're less inclined to have to prove anything to anybody. A lot came from my kitchen, where I finally started paying attention to what was literally in front of me. Not where I *was*, or where I wanted to go—and this, in these electronics-driven times, is becoming increasingly difficult. (Our brain's capacity to remain present, plugged into our surroundings and not our devices, is literally shrinking.)

Strangely enough, the more mind*ful* I am about food, the less mind-space I *give* it—that's right, what I give it, not what it *takes*. I am no longer distracted by dieting, battling food, controlling cravings, and blood sugar swings. It is incredibly freeing. Spoiler alert: conscious eating (and cooking) doesn't fix everything. Sorry. But, it lets you look at some other stuff that could use your attention. Imagine, for a second, making peace with food, and that Western word, modified: *happierness*.

In both of my cultures, for as far back as we have records (think Paleo), meat, in some form, makes the dish "main." Is it necessary? No. Is it good for you? Depends. What "we" (I mean "they," the

scientific and medical powers that be) know is that "*fast*" carbs are bad for you. It is difficult to isolate meat eating from other dietary and other lifestyle habits, such as exercise, smoking, overeating, etc. All other things being equal, the few comparative studies of Paleotarians and vegetarians show no added or decreased benefit to consuming meat. Let's backpedal one word: by meat, they mean unprocessed, relatively good quality meat cooked at a low temperature (in the oven or on the stove, not grilled), and making up roughly 25 percent of what's on your plate (they'll let you include your salad plate, if it's separate, but not dessert).

I've culled the best of my best so-called "mains"—the ones that get the most guest requests. Get ready, the person/people with whom you share your table (the industrious ones, anyway) will ask for your recipes. When was the last time that happened with "diet food"? Thank the fisherman. I remember getting into the car that night and sighing, *Upakaaram*. Roughly translated, *thank you*, but word-for-word, *it has been a great favor*.

Reema and her cute son Rohan, Tomj, Deepa

*Bay of Bengal, Arabian Sea, and the Indian Ocean

Ammachi's Clay Pot Fish Molee

Ammachi's clay pots had a well-loved patina that came from years of use, more beautiful than any finish I've ever seen. An Indian molee is a stew made with coconut milk. Hers would have simmered on the wood stove for hours. Yours will be ready in thirty minutes!

SERVES 4

1 lb halibut or your favorite fish, cut into 2-inch cubes

¼ teaspoon turmeric
½ teaspoon cayenne powder
2 teaspoons Deepa's Secret Spice (or substitute Quick Mix Fish, p. 24)
1 teaspoon salt

3 tablespoons unrefined coconut oil
1 teaspoon black mustard seeds
2 shallots, finely minced
10 fresh curry leaves
2 tablespoons Ginger Garlic Paste (p. 38)
1 jalapeño, slit with the top intact
4 black peppercorns
2 small tomatoes, chopped
2 tablespoons fresh lemon juice
1 can (14 oz) unsweetened coconut milk

Crowning flavor:
2 tablespoons Caramelized Shallots (p. 58)

1 sprig curry leaves

1. Dust fish with turmeric, cayenne powder, Deepa's Secret Spice, and salt, and set aside.

2. Heat oil in a deep 12-inch saucepan over medium-high heat until it shimmers (about two minutes). Drop a few mustard seeds in first and wait a bit if they don't pop right away before adding all the mustard seeds (shield yourself with lid as the seeds will pop). Add shallots and stir until golden brown (approximately one minute).

3. Reduce heat and add curry leaves, Ginger Garlic Paste, jalapeño, and black peppercorns. Stir and move this mixture to the edges of the pan. Place fish in the middle in a single layer directly on the pan. Cook undisturbed for 4 minutes to lightly brown the fish.

4. Gently turn fish over and add tomatoes with lemon juice. Cover and cook for 3 minutes.

5. Add coconut milk (I discard any clear liquid in the can and just use the thick milk part). Simmer (without boiling), uncovered, for 3 minutes. Check seasoning.

Crowning flavor: Tasty but optional: Sprinkle Caramelized Shallots on top. Garnish with the whole sprig of curry leaves, when serving family style.

Serve over or alongside whole grain—Gingered Farro with Dried Fruit and Nuts (p. 64), accompanied by Cauliflower and Beans Tumble (p. 138) and Peppery Papadum (p. 62).

DEEPA'S SECRET

If you are out of Deepa's Secret Spice (or time), you could use the alternate mix (for fish) in the Deepa's Secret Spice recipe on (p. 24).

Black mustard seed: *The mustard plant is a crucifer belonging to the same family as Brussels sprouts and cauliflower. The tiny seed has the same nutrients and properties in concentrated form. It can help lower the risk of diabetes and heart disease, and it is full of antioxidants.*

Aromatic Fish in Parchment

We ate a lot of pomfret, an Indian sea fish, when I was growing up. I've only ever seen it frozen in a couple of Asian markets here. I miss it! Any lean, firm, fresh fish will work beautifully in parchment. Black cod or halibut are equally delicious.

SERVES 4

1–1½ lbs black cod or halibut, cut into 4 pieces of 4-inch squares

Dusting mix:
¼ teaspoon turmeric
¼ teaspoon cayenne powder
¼ teaspoon allspice
¼ teaspoon dried thyme
1 teaspoon salt
¼ teaspoon fresh ground black pepper

4 parchment paper squares (approximately 12-inch squares)

Condiments:
4 cloves, smashed
4 garlic cloves, ground to a paste
1 shallot, sliced thin
1 tablespoon ginger, slivered (you can leave skin on)
8 curry leaves

4 tablespoons unrefined coconut oil, melted over low heat
4 lemon slices (¼-inch thick)
4 jalapeños, slit in half lengthwise with the top intact

Crowning flavor:
2 tablespoons New Indian Gremolata (p. 60)

Make ahead: Parchment bundles can be prepared hours ahead of time.

1. Preheat oven to 400°F.

2. Pat the fish dry with a paper towel and dust with dusting mix.

3. Place parchment squares on baking sheet. Mix the condiments and divide among the four squares.

4. Place fish on top of the condiments in the middle of the parchment squares. Drizzle with coconut oil. Top each piece of fish with a lemon slice and jalapeño.

5. Fold parchment paper like an envelope, tucking two open ends under the fish bundle.

6. Sear parchment bundles in the hot oven (twelve minutes).

7. I like to serve the fish on a platter, still sitting in the parchment paper that I cooked the fish in (just unwrapped). If you prefer, you could remove from parchment paper and plate.

Crowning flavor: Sprinkle fish with New Indian Gremolata before serving for a boost of fresh flavor.

Start with Deepaganoush on Endive (p. 108) and fill out the plate with Best-Ever Oven-Roasted Swee' Potato Fries (p. 132).

DEEPA'S SECRET

Cooking in parchment is a French steaming technique, which seals in food's (meats and vegetables) moistness and flavor. Serve in parchment at an adventurous table— or remove from parchment before plating.

Dilled Masala Crab Cakes

Some form of starch—flour, potato, cornstarch—typically holds crab cakes together. Mine are all fish— I use mashed shrimp to bind the cakes. The crushed potato chip coating gives your crab cakes an irresistible crunch.

SERVES 4

Chop and mix ingredients:
1 tablespoon green onion
2 tablespoons shallots
1 tablespoon garlic
½ tablespoon jalapeño
¼ teaspoon ground fennel
½ teaspoon garam masala
½ teaspoon ground allspice
1 tablespoon fresh dill, finely chopped
1 teaspoon chaat masala
1 egg, beaten
1 tablespoon fresh lemon juice
Zest of 1 lemon
1 teaspoon salt
½ teaspoon fresh ground black pepper

¼ lb shrimp, shelled and deveined
1 lb lump crab meat, cooked
(Dungeness, if you can get it)

Crust:
2 cups potato chips, crushed

1 tablespoon unrefined coconut oil
(melted over low heat)

Edible flower petals (optional)

1. Turn broiler on.

2. In a food processor, pulse chop and mix ingredients into a chunky puree, *not* paste. Add shrimp and pulse. You want a chunky consistency.

3. Fold in crab meat gently. Form crab and shrimp mixture into 6–8 crab cakes (approximately 2½-inch rounds).

4. Put the crushed potato chips on a large pie plate or platter. Gently press the crab patties into the crushed potato chips, covering the top, bottom, and sides.

5. Place the patties (without crowding) on a baking tray lined with parchment paper.

6. Top each patty with a ¼ teaspoon of coconut oil and broil for 2–3 minutes unil lightly browned. No need to flip over. (The crab meat is already cooked and rough chopped shrimp cooks fast. Careful not to overcook as it will get tough.)

7. Serve browned side up, topped with edible flower petals. Chutput Ketchup (p. 36), Reemsie's Tamarind Sauce (p. 34), or any savory sauce of your choosing makes a good dip.

Crab cakes pair well with Ginger Cabbage Slaw (p. 122) and Dryfoossels Sprouts (p. 144).

Dill: *Although fresh dill weed is not in the Ayurvedic doctor's kit, it has been used for medicinal purposes in other parts of Southeast Asia for centuries. It can help lower cholesterol, aid digestion, and prevent infection and inflammation.*

A Tangle of Crab Legs in Savory Coconut Cream

SERVES 4

2 tablespoons unrefined coconut oil

1 teaspoon mustard seeds

1 teaspoon (Lucknow) fennel seeds

10 curry leaves

4 cups leeks, cleaned and finely chopped

1 tablespoon garlic paste

1 tablespoon ginger, freshly grated (skin-on is fine)

2 tomatoes, quartered

1 teaspoon dried thyme

½ teaspoon cayenne flakes

2 tablespoons vinegar, apricot or white balsamic

1 teaspoon salt

½ teaspoon fresh ground black pepper

4 cups unsweetened coconut milk

1 lb fresh (cooked and shelled) crab legs

1 cup parsley, finely chopped, for garnish

*I suggest **Native Forest unsweetened coconut milk** because it is the closest thing to pure coconut milk. Please do not use "lite" coconut milk as it is diluted with more water and likely has preservatives.*

For centuries, Kerala, the spice and condiment capital of the world, was a hub on the East-West trading route. We may never know whether the Portuguese introduced the use of fresh coconut milk (infused with cloves, cinnamon, sautéed shallots, curry leaves, garlic, and ginger) as a base for fish and vegetable stews—or took it with them back in the fifteenth century. Thampy and I loved the familiarity of the savory coconut cream sauce we discovered on our visit to Brazil in the eighties. This savory coconut cream achieves the same great flavor with far fewer steps than the traditional method. Go ahead and use my coconut cream sauce for other meat, fish, or vegetable dishes for what is known as molee flavor, the taste of Kerala (not to be confused with mole, the chocolate-based sauce from Mexico).

Make ahead: You can make the sauce ahead of time (steps 1–3) and store in refrigerator overnight.

1. Heat oil in a heavy 14-inch skillet until shimmering (it takes a couple of minutes).

2. Add mustard and fennel seeds and curry leaves, being careful to shield yourself from sputtering with a lid. Add leeks, lower heat, and cook, stirring, for about 5 minutes until leeks soften—don't brown.

3. Add garlic, ginger, and tomatoes. Stir for one minute. Add thyme, cayenne flakes, vinegar, salt, and pepper. Mix well, then add coconut milk. Dilute with water, if necessary, for preferred sauce consistency. Check seasoning.

4. Add crab. Remove from heat. Let the crab sit on the sauce. It looks pretty served this way. Accent with a burst of bright green chopped parsley.

DEEPA'S SECRET

To clean leeks, remove the root end of the bulb and the tougher dark green ends. (You will use the white and light green parts only.) Fill a clean bowl with cold water. Chop in ½-inch pieces and add to the bowl. Swirl to release sand and dirt. (It will fall to the bottom.) Remove with a slotted spoon or strainer.

Making coconut milk from scratch: In a blender, add 2 cups of frozen shredded coconut (available at Whole Foods and Indian supermarkets). Add 4–5 cups of warm water and blend for 2 minutes. Strain the coconut milk through a colander (lined with cheese cloth) into a glass bowl. Squeeze the cheese cloth to get the creamy part of the coconut milk.

Kerala Fisherman's Prawns

SERVES 4

2 lbs large prawns, shelled and deveined

2 tablespoons Ginger Garlic Paste (p. 38)
3 Malabar fish tamarind, available
    online, halved lengthwise (or ½ cup
    fresh lemon juice)
¼ cup water

Dried spices:
½ teaspoon cayenne powder
½ teaspoon turmeric
1 teaspoon paprika
½ teaspoon asafoetida
¼ teaspoon garam masala
¼ teaspoon ground coriander
1 teaspoon salt
1 teaspoon fresh ground black pepper

3 tablespoons unrefined coconut oil
½ cup shallots, finely chopped
¼ cup red onion, finely chopped
10 curry leaves

Crowning flavor:
1 cup Caramelized Shallots (p. 58)

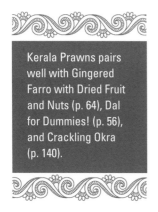

Kerala Prawns pairs well with Gingered Farro with Dried Fruit and Nuts (p. 64), Dal for Dummies! (p. 56), and Crackling Okra (p. 140).

In New Delhi, we'd get our fish on Sundays on the way home from church. My dad would pull up to the fish market and my mother would jump out in her Sunday best. We'd watch her haggle with the fisherman as the newspaper-wrapped bundles piled up. Then she'd drop them in the trunk—my father wouldn't let her keep the fish in the front (his car was his prized possession)—and the three of us, all dressed up, took up the entire backseat.

1. Mix cleaned prawns with Ginger Garlic Paste, Kerala fish tamarind (also called Malabar Tamarind or *Kudampuli*), ¼ cup of water, and the dried spices in a glass or ceramic bowl. Marinate prawns (covered, in the fridge overnight or at room temperature for half an hour). If you are using lemon juice, do not add until step 5.

2. Heat oil in a wok or large skillet (give the prawns plenty of room) over medium-high heat.

3. Add finely chopped shallots and onion. When shallots and onion begin to brown, add curry leaves. (Shield yourself with a lid as curry leaves could splutter!) When the shallots and onion are light brown, remove half the mixture and set aside.

4. Add marinating prawns to the pan and cook, stirring occasionally, for 6–8 minutes. The prawns should be coated in a yummy reduction (water will have evaporated and sauce will have thickened).

5. Add lemon juice (if substituted for Kerala fish tamarind) and mix well. Remove from heat. Check seasoning.

Crowning flavor: Top the prawns with the reserved browned onion and curry leaves. Optional: I add a layer of Caramelized Shallots. The combination of browned onion and caramelized shallots is extra-deca-delicious.

Malabar Tamarind (Kudampuli): Kudampuli is the gnarly dried rind of the wild mangosteen, a variety of fruit indigenous to Kerala. The sweet-and-sour taste is unique, but Kudampuli was seldom seen outside of India until Dr. Oz touted its potential for weight loss. The studies are not conclusive. However, the garcinol compound in Kudampuli has both antioxidant and anti-inflammatory properties. Ayurvedic doctors traditionally used Kudampuli to treat stomach ulcers.

Nawabi Tuna Kebab Burger

These hand packed fish patties take the burger up a notch. Flash-fried, they're still moist inside. Indulge yourself or your guests (Nawabs were Ottoman nobility, after all), and serve them with one or more of your favorite sauces.

SERVES 4

Dipping sauce:
4 tablespoons sriracha sauce
2 tablespoons fresh lemon juice
½ shallot, minced
1 garlic clove, minced

1 lb fresh tuna, salmon, or halibut;
    skinned, filleted, and cut into cubes

Fresh ingredients:
1 shallot, rough chopped
1 garlic clove
1 jalapeño, seeded for less heat and
    chopped
2 tablespoons cilantro leaves, stemmed
    and finely chopped
1 tablespoon mint leaves, stemmed and
    finely chopped
½ teaspoon dried thyme
2 tablespoons lemon zest (approximately
    2 lemons)
1 tablespoon fresh lemon juice
1 teaspoon fresh ginger, grated

Dried spices:
¼ teaspoon fennel seeds, toasted
2 cloves
¼ teaspoon allspice
¼ teaspoon cayenne powder
½ teaspoon fresh ground pepper
½ teaspoon salt

1 egg, beaten
1 cup unrefined coconut oil (1 inch of oil
    in your frying pan)

Make ahead: You can refrigerate or freeze uncooked burger patties to defrost, cook, and serve later.

1. Preheat oven to 375°F (for well-done kebabs).

2. Mix the dipping sauce ingredients in a blender and set aside. Check seasoning.

3. In a food processor, pulse fish with fresh ingredients to a rough (ground beef) consistency. Transfer to a glass bowl.

4. Grind the dried spices. Gently stir into the fish mixture and add the beaten egg.

5. Shape the fish mixture into burger-size patties.

6. Heat unrefined coconut oil in a skillet (large enough to hold patties without crowding). You need 1 inch of oil in your frying pan. When oil is shimmering, fry burgers until both sides are golden brown (about two minutes per side).

7. For well-done burgers, finish in the hot oven for about four minutes.

8. Serve hot with dipping sauce and/or any of my other sauces.

Nawabi Tuna Kebab Burger with Tousled Haricots Verts and Caramelized Carrots (p. 154) and Avocado, Tomato, and Plum Salad (p. 116).

Clove: The Spice Wars in the early 1600s were fought over the clove. The oil of clove is a mild analgesic, which also has circulatory and anti-inflammatory benefits, and was the dentist's drug of choice for pain relief, long before there were drugs to choose from.

General Joseph's Five-Star Chicken Batons

On the occasions when General Joseph was in uniform, his chest was covered in medals. Uncle Joseph was a surgeon and head of the Armed Forces Medical Corps. He would operate in the morning—his were the most difficult cases—and arrive home for "lunch" at 3 or 4 p.m. His workday was technically done, but we wouldn't see him again until late that night, after he had checked in on each of his patients one more time. I would have loved to serve him his namesake chicken skewers to go with his nightcap.

SERVES 4

2 boneless chicken breasts

Marinade:
1 tablespoon toasted sesame oil
2 tablespoons fresh lemon juice
3 tablespoons Ginger Garlic Paste (p. 38)
2 tablespoons shallots, minced in a food
    processor
1 slice bacon, finely chopped
1 teaspoon cayenne powder
½ teaspoon turmeric
1 teaspoon salt
1 teaspoon garam masala
1 teaspoon allspice
2–3 drops liquid smoke

8 six-inch skewers, wooden (soaked in
    water for one hour) or metal
2 tablespoons toasted sesame oil, for
    basting
1 tablespoon chaat masala

Make ahead: If you are using wooden skewers, you will need to soak them in water for an hour before using. Meanwhile, your chicken can be marinating—at least an hour or overnight, in the fridge. Uncooked chicken skewers freeze and defrost well.

1. Pound chicken breast between two sheets of parchment paper with wooden mallet until ½-inch thick. Cut into 1-inch strips.

2. Mix the marinade in a medium glass bowl. Add chicken, cover, and hold in the fridge for at least one hour.

3. Position rack in middle of oven and turn broiler on.

4. Thread chicken on skewers. Brush with sesame oil and broil, 5 minutes per side.

5. Sprinkle with chaat masala and serve hot with Deepa's Green Sauce (p. 30) or Chutput Ketchup (p. 36) for delicious dipping.

You could pair this dish with New Indian Pesto and Bean Soup (p. 94) and Avocado, Tomato and Plum Salad (p. 116). An obvious main dish, the chicken skewers are also popular starters.

DEEPA'S SECRET
You can get great grilled flavor from a few drops of liquid smoke. I prefer Lazy Kettle Brand, All Natural Hickory Liquid Smoke.

New Indian Cacciatore

SERVES 4

8 chicken thighs

Seasoning:
1 teaspoon salt
1 teaspoon fresh ground black pepper
½ teaspoon turmeric
½ teaspoon cayenne powder
½ teaspoon paprika

2 tablespoons unrefined coconut oil
    (divided)
½ teaspoon fennel seeds
8 sage leaves

4 shallots, finely chopped
4 teaspoons Ginger Garlic Paste (p. 38)
1 tablespoon Deepa's Secret Spice (or
    substitute Quick Mix Meat, p. 24)
2 medium tomatoes, chopped
1 cup dry white wine (optional)
2 cups water (or 3 cups water if not
    using wine)
1 teaspoon salt

1 teaspoon fresh rosemary leaves,
    chopped
1 tablespoon fresh lemon juice

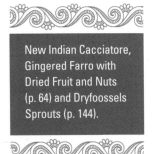

New Indian Cacciatore,
Gingered Farro with
Dried Fruit and Nuts
(p. 64) and Dryfoossels
Sprouts (p. 144).

Rosemary: *Traditional healers have always believed that the fragrant woody stems have special curative powers. Just breathing the scent produced by rosemary oil can reduce stress and is said to enhance memory.*

We used to call this "Don't Fight with the Chicken" chicken. My restaurateur friend Ralph taught me to panfry chicken before roasting it in the oven. You have to let it sit on the heat a full 5 to 8 minutes. "Don't fight with it, Deepa! It will release when it's ready." I quit fighting. Okay, I still make the occasional prod with my spatula, but Ralph's right—leave it alone.

Make ahead: You can prepare the whole dish up to 24 hours ahead of time; just take care of your chicken skin. Make sure it's not submerged, and re-crisp by broiling 30 seconds after reheating.

1. Preheat oven to 350°F.

2. Pat the chicken dry. Mix seasoning ingredients. Sprinkle evenly over chicken pieces.

3. Heat a 10-inch cast iron skillet or other large, heavy, ovenproof pan. Add 1 tablespoon of oil. When oil is shimmering, add fennel seeds and place the chicken skin-side down, and leave it be. The chicken should release from the pan with the gentle nudge of a spatula (5–8 minutes). If it doesn't, don't fight with it, it will release when it is ready! Flip over and cook for 2 minutes on the other side.

4. Transfer chicken to a plate. Add the remaining tablespoon of oil to the pan. Crisp the sage leaves in oil (about a minute), then remove and set aside for garnish later.

5. In the same pan, brown the shallots until golden (about 6 minutes). Add Ginger Garlic Paste and stir for 30 seconds, until fragrant. Add Deepa's Secret Spice and stir for one minute. Add chopped tomatoes and cook covered for one minute. Add wine, water, and 1 teaspoon salt. Stir well.

6. Return the chicken to the pan, skin-side up. Make sure chicken is not fully submerged to keep the skin crisp. Bake uncovered for 45 minutes. If cacciatore bubbles, lower temperature to 300°F.

7. Transfer chicken skin side up to serving platter. Reduce the remaining pan liquid by half on the stove, over medium heat (about 3 minutes). Remove from heat, add rosemary leaves and lemon juice. Pour the reduced sauce over the chicken and garnish with crisped sage leaves.

DEEPA'S SECRET

If you're out of Deepa's Secret Spice (or time), substitute the alternate spice mix (for meat) in the Deepa's Secret Spice recipe.

Mary's Famous "Cutlets" (Meatballs)

I know, how did I get from "cutlets" to meatballs. In a word, taste! To begin with, my mother's were "British" cutlets, which are something like croquettes or patties rolled in breadcrumbs (not the American cut of meat). All the flavor in my recipe is packed into smaller parcels, which keep their shape without the breadcrumbs. Mary's Famous's fans would approve.

SERVES 4

2 small potatoes
4 tablespoons unrefined coconut oil (divided)
4 shallots, finely chopped
6 curry leaves
3 garlic cloves, minced
½-inch piece fresh ginger (unpeeled), minced
½ celery stalk, finely chopped
½ carrot, finely chopped

Ground spices:
1 teaspoon coriander seeds, toasted and ground
8 black peppercorns, toasted and ground
½ teaspoon cumin seeds, toasted and ground
¼ teaspoon cinnamon
¼ teaspoon cardamom
¼ teaspoon ground cloves
¼ teaspoon garam masala
2 teaspoons salt

1 tablespoon fresh tomato, finely chopped
1 lb ground lamb or sirloin
1 cup fresh cilantro, chopped

2 eggs
1 teaspoon Worcestershire sauce (I like Lea and Perrins)

Crowning flavor:
1 cup New Indian Gremolata (p. 60)
1 tablespoon fresh lemon juice

Make ahead: It will speed up the process if you have mashed potatoes on hand. Peel two small potatoes, boil, and mash.

1. Heat 2 tablespoons of unrefined coconut oil in a heavy 10-inch skillet over medium heat. Add shallots and brown until golden color (about 5 minutes). Add curry leaves, garlic, ginger, celery, and carrot. Sauté until celery and carrot begin to soften (about 2 minutes).

2. Add ground spices. Cook for one minute, stirring. Add tomato and sauté for one minute. Careful not to burn! Remove from heat and add mashed potato and meat. Stir in cilantro leaves (save a few leaves for garnish).

3. Beat eggs with Worcestershire sauce and add to meat mixture. Remove curry leaves. Form into 2-inch balls and refrigerate for at least one hour (helps meatballs keep their shape) or freeze (and defrost) until ready to cook.

4. Preheat oven to 200°F to keep cooked meatballs warm.

5. Heat remaining 2 tablespoons of oil in a heavy skillet. Gently lower meatballs into hot pan without crowding. Cook in batches, turning meatballs carefully until golden brown (rare to well done, your choice). Transfer to baking sheet and place in warm oven. Continue until all meatballs are cooked. (You may need to add more oil.)

Crowning flavor: Top with New Indian Gremolata. Serve with Chutput Ketchup (p. 36) for dipping or on a puddle of Chukku's Yogurt Salad (p. 124).

Mary's Famous "Cutlets" (Meatballs) with Oatmeal Uppma (p. 70) and Aviel (p. 130).

Coconut oil *is nature's richest source of medium chain fatty acids. By contrast, most common vegetable or seed oils are comprised of long chain fatty acids. It is difficult for the body to break down these large molecules and they are predominantly stored as fat. Being smaller, medium chain fatty acids are more easily digested and immediately burned by liver for energy—like carbohydrates, but without the insulin spike. The medium chain fatty acids boost the metabolism and help the body use fat for energy, as opposed to storing it, so it can actually help you become leaner.*

Chop Chop Lamb Chops

SERVES 4

8–10 lamb chops, "Frenched" (ask a
friendly butcher to "French" your
chops or use a sharp knife to strip
away fat to expose the long bone,
leaving a "lollipop" shaped meat on
top)

Marinade:
4 shallots, thinly sliced
20 curry leaves
2 small tomatoes, quartered
3 tablespoons white vinegar (or ¼ cup
fresh lemon juice)
5 teaspoons Deepa's Secret Spice (p. 24)
(or substitute Quick Mix Meat)
3 tablespoons Ginger Garlic Paste (p. 38)
3 tablespoons unrefined coconut oil
(melted over low heat) or extra virgin
olive oil
1 teaspoon salt
1 teaspoon fresh ground black pepper

Crowning flavor:
3 tablespoons balsamic vinegar
2 tablespoons cilantro leaves, stemmed
and finely chopped
2 tablespoons mint leaves, stemmed and
finely chopped
2 tablespoons basil leaves, stemmed
and finely chopped
Sprig curry leaves

We didn't eat lamb when I was a kid. There was "mutton" (goat)
occasionally, but it was expensive and had to be cooked until it was
falling off its old bones. (Beef was actually the least expensive meat, then
chicken.) Here, your pan-to-plate time is less than ten minutes.

Make ahead: You can marinate lamb chops in fridge up to 24 hours
ahead of time. Bring to room temperature (sit out for one hour) before
pan-roasting.

1. Preheat oven to 375°F (for medium to well-done chops).

2. Mix marinade in large glass bowl.

3. Rub marinade into the chops. Cover and leave at room temperature for
an hour.

4. Heat a heavy oven-proof skillet and brown chops in a single layer over
high heat for 3 minutes (the oil is already in the marinade). Flip and
brown for 2 minutes for medium doneness. For medium-well, you
could finish the chops in the oven for 5 minutes.

5. Serve naked (the chops, I mean) with Deepa's Green Sauce (p. 30) if
you like.

Crowning flavor: Drizzle the balsamic vinegar, with a quick movement
of your hand, on the cooked lamb chops. Garnish with chopped cilantro,
mint, and basil. A sprig of curry leaves makes a beautiful garnish.

*Disappearing leftovers: Give
your colleagues lunch envy; brown
bag your leftovers. Or cube lamb
chops and add to whole grain
pilafs. Truth is, these chops usually
disappear, period, no leftovers.
Make extra and hide them.*

Feeling fancy? Serve
Tomato Rasam (p. 92)
as a starter, in teacups.
Follow with Chop
Chop Lamb Chops as
an entrée. Tousled
Haricots Verts and
Caramelized Carrots
(p. 154) or Ralph's
Garlicky Spinach a la
Dal (p. 142) are good
pairings with lamb
chops. And save room
for dessert—a bowl
of Mango Lassi (p. 194)
with fresh mango
slices on top.

Tomji's Spicy Kerala Beef with Coconut Chips

My brother Tomji, a well-known wildlife conservationist, is also a carnivore. People in Kerala call this preparation *Erachi Olarthya* or beef roast with fresh coconut chips. Tomji will literally sing for this supper—with his distinctive baritone crooning his signature "Mona Lisa," he gives Nat King Cole a run for his money! If my big brother didn't live so far away, I'd make it for him all the time.

Make ahead: Deepa's Secret Spice (p. 24). Try to have this spice mix on hand ahead of time.

1. In a food processor, blend marinade ingredients to a paste.

2. Mix meat and coconut chips with the marinade in a large glass bowl. Cover and set aside for at least 30 minutes at room temp or up to 24 hours in the fridge. (Bring to room temperature before cooking.)

3. Cook the marinated meat and coconut chips in a covered heavy 4-quart saucepan over medium heat for 30 minutes.

4. *Tadka:* Meanwhile, heat oil in a 10-inch skillet or wok over medium heat until shimmering. Drop a couple of mustard seeds in the oil; if seeds do not splutter, continue heating oil and try again.

5. Shield yourself with a lid as you add jalapeño and curry leaves. Sauté for one minute. Transfer jalapeno and curry leaves onto a small plate with a slotted spoon to use for garnish later. Add mustard and fennel seeds to the skillet. When they begin to pop, add the onions. Brown the onions until golden.

6. Add roasting ingredients and sauté for one minute.

7. Stir in cooked meat and coconut chips and cook over medium heat for 10 minutes. Remove from the heat.

8. Stir in lemon juice. Check seasoning and garnish with the reserved jalapeño and curry leaves.

SERVES 4

Marinade:
3 whole dried red chili peppers (dry roasted)
½ teaspoon turmeric
10 curry leaves
1 tablespoon coriander seeds, toasted and ground
1 tablespoon garam masala
1 cup water
1 tablespoon white vinegar
5 garlic cloves
1-inch piece fresh ginger, grated (un-peeled is fine)
1 cup onions, sliced
1 teaspoon salt
1 teaspoon fresh ground pepper

1½ lbs beef stew meat in 2-inch cubes (Try American Kobe, it's worth it!)
2 cups coconut chips (frozen coconut chips are available at most Indian grocery stores)

Tadka:
4 tablespoons unrefined coconut oil
1 tablespoon mustard seeds
2 jalapeño peppers, quartered length-wise
10 curry leaves
1 teaspoon fennel seeds
2 medium onions, thinly sliced

Roasting ingredients:
3 garlic cloves, smashed and chopped
1 tablespoon ginger, slivered
2 teaspoons Deepa's Secret Spice (p. 24) (or substitute Quick Mix Meat)
1 teaspoon salt
1 tomato, quartered
1 tablespoon fresh lemon juice

Serve warm with Heritage Barley (Better Than Rice) Pilaf (p. 66), Chukku's Yogurt Salad (p. 124), Peppery Papadum (p. 62) and Crackling Okra (p. 140).

DEEPA'S SECRET

If you're out of Deepa's Secret Spice (or time), substitute the alternate spice mix (for meat) in the Deepa's Secret Spice recipe.

Tomato: *The tomato is a fruit (not a vegetable) full of lycopene, an antioxidant that lowers the risk of diabetes and heart disease.*

Keema Spicy Beef

This was our grad student go-to dinner, back in the day. Quick, delicious, good for two or a whole gaggle of students in need of a flavorful and wallet-friendly meal. Forty years later, it never gets old . . .

SERVES 6

Fresh spices:
½-inch fresh ginger, grated
4 garlic cloves, smashed
1 cup canned whole tomato (with juice)
1 tablespoon vinegar (I recommend fruit vinegar), apricot or plum
1 tablespoon salt
½ teaspoon fresh ground black pepper

2 tablespoons unrefined coconut oil (divided)
1 red onion, rough chopped
1 jalapeño, slit into 4 with the top intact

Dried spices:
6 black peppercorns
½-inch cinnamon stick
4 cardamom pods
1 teaspoon turmeric
1 teaspoon garam masala
1 teaspoon coriander seeds
1 teaspoon paprika
1 teaspoon cayenne flakes
4 cloves
1 teaspoon cumin seeds
1 teaspoon fennel seeds
1 star anise
1 black cardamom pod
2 bay leaves

Vegetables:
½ cup carrot, cut into 1-inch pieces
½ cup bell pepper, cut into 1-inch squares
½ cup leek, chopped
½ cup potato (or turnip), peeled and cut into 1-inch cubes

1 lb ground beef or lamb
1 bunch mint, stemmed and rough chopped
1 bunch cilantro, stemmed and rough chopped

Crowning flavor:
1 cup New Indian Gremolata (p. 60)

Make ahead: Keema, prepared ahead of time or leftover, keeps well in fridge or freezer.

1. Puree the fresh spices in a blender, and add salt and pepper. Set aside.

2. Heat 1 tablespoon of oil in a 14-inch heavy-bottomed pan or wok over medium heat. Brown onion and jalapeño for 6 minutes. Remove and set aside for topping later.

3. In the same pan, heat remaining 1 tablespoon of oil and add the dried spices, vegetables, and meat. Brown the meat and vegetables on high heat for 5 minutes, stirring to break up clumps.

4. Add the blended fresh spices to the browned meat and vegetables. Cover and cook until vegetables are al dente (about 8 minutes). Remove from heat and stir in chopped mint and cilantro leaves. Check seasoning.

Crowning flavor: Top with the browned onion and jalapeño that you set aside in step 2. Garnish with New Indian Gremolata.

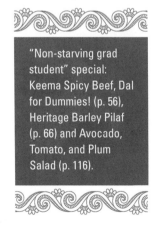

"Non-starving grad student" special: Keema Spicy Beef, Dal for Dummies! (p. 56), Heritage Barley Pilaf (p. 66) and Avocado, Tomato, and Plum Salad (p. 116).

Disappearing Leftovers: Mix whole grain pasta with keema for a good-as-new meal the next day! Drizzle with extra virgin olive oil and sprinkle some asiago cheese.

DEEPA'S SECRET
I hardly ever peel ginger, and you don't need to either unless the skin is really thick and tough. The nutrients are concentrated in the skin.

Truck Stop Pork Chops

The world over, truckers home in on good food! This is particularly true in India where unpretentious rest-stop eateries serve up some of the most elegantly-flavored pork chops! Here is my take on the Indian roadside classic. You can brine and "rub" ahead of time, but don't let the cooked chops sit too long—they're best eaten just out of the oven.

SERVES 4

Brining ingredients:
6 cups water
¼ cup salt
¼ teaspoon allspice berries
4 cloves
¼ teaspoon cayenne flakes
1 star anise
2 tablespoons dark brown sugar
1 teaspoon (Lucknow) fennel seeds
1 tablespoon black peppercorns
1 bay leaf
2 tablespoons apple cider vinegar
2 garlic cloves, smashed

4 pork chops (1-inch to 1½-inch thick)

Dried spice rub:
¼ teaspoon ground cumin
¼ teaspoon thyme
¼ teaspoon oregano
¼ teaspoon garam masala
¼ teaspoon paprika
¼ teaspoon dark brown sugar
¼ teaspoon cayenne flakes

2–3 drops liquid smoke (Lazy Kettle Brand All Natural Hickory Liquid Smoke)
1 tablespoon unrefined coconut oil (to glaze the cast-iron skillet in which you will cook the chops)

Crowning flavor:
1 cup New Indian Gremolata (p. 60)

Make ahead: You'll need at least two hours to brine and one hour for the rub to flavor your pork chops. (Cook time is less than one half hour.)

1. Brining liquid: In a large saucepan, bring all the brining ingredients to a boil. Remove from heat, cover, and cool.

2. Place pork chops in a lidded glass container. Pour cooled brining liquid over chops to submerge. Cover and refrigerate 2 hours, or overnight.

3. One hour before cooking, rinse pork chops in cold water and pat dry with paper towels. Dust with dried spice rub, sprinkle with liquid smoke, and set aside.

4. Preheat oven to 450°F (used only for medium and well-done chops).

5. Meanwhile, heat oil in a cast-iron skillet or any heavy-bottomed ovenproof skillet on the stove. Cook pork chops in a single layer (do not crowd) over high heat until slightly charred, 2 minutes per side. Chops will be medium rare.

6. For more medium or well-done, finish roasting in the oven, about 3 minutes (150°F–160°F internal temperature for medium). Tent with foil and allow cooked chops to rest for five minutes before serving.

Crowning flavor: Garnish with New Indian Gremolata and serve.

Your Truck Stop Pork Chops go with at least two sides: Hot 'n' Crispy Cabbage (p. 150) and Kala Chola Salad (p. 120).

Star Anise *is the most beautiful spice on the shelf. The eight-pointed star is the signature spice of Chinese cuisine, and a pillar of traditional Chinese medicine. Star anise and its compounds are used to treat the flu and it is said to inhibit other viruses.*

"*I will be waiting in the wings.*"

—Miss Ruth Compton

11

Sweet Endings

Mango Lassi
Toot Sweet

Sweet Endings

After my mother died, my dad came for an extended visit to our home in Woodside. A man who had little time for pastimes (except chess), he had amassed a sizable library for his retirement. Sadly, macular degeneration robbed him of his eyesight. It was my privilege and real pleasure to read these books aloud each afternoon to the man who gave me my love of literature.

I was still holding Richard Feynman's biography, *Genius*, on my lap minutes after we'd finished our chapter when I finally asked him the question. Not why (even I could see it was the right thing to do, especially after I had sons of my own), but how: "*Dada*, how could you send me to boarding school, five hundred miles away?"

He looked away, as if his eyes might not have been capable of meeting mine. "I had to, your mother did not understand you." My brother and sister were academic achievers, numbers one and two in their respective classes. *Amma* never understood why I wasn't "smart" like them. When I finished eighth grade, *Dada* withdrew me from the New Delhi Carmel Convent and enrolled me in Miss Compton's All Saints boarding school, which had done well by his close friends' daughters. He literally invested half a month's pay in my education—they only ate meat once a week during those years, (It makes me feel better when I think it was probably marginal quality meat that was unhealthily high in saturated fats).

My portrait of *Dada*

All Saints was a British boarding school in the foothills of the Himalayas. After a day-and-night's train ride, I was handed the school's blue serge uniform and matching blazer. Twelve years old, I was no longer Deepa, my father's light; I was Elizabeth, my Christian name. In those first few weeks, I kept to myself; as Miss Compton's regular correspondence with my father recounts, I was not "mixing well."

"Who would like to recite a poem at our next morning assembly?" Miss Compton surveyed the chapel's pews at the all-school gathering. No hands. "Elizabeth Mathew. Thank you. I will share the poem with you in my office forthwith."

"Miss Compton, I can't," I blurted out, staring down at her desk. I would throw up onstage, sealing my future as an outcast at All Saints (all saints that is, but me).

"Elizabeth, we will do it together." She handed me a copy of Wordsworth's "Daffodils." "I will be waiting in the wings."

ALL SAINTS' SCHOOL
NAINI TAL, U.P.

PRINCIPAL, MISS R. K. COMPTON, M.A. (OXON)
TELEPHONE NO. 41.

18ᵗʰ Dec. 1972

Dear Elizabeth,

Have a very happy day and a very happy married life!

Your lovely long letters deserve a long answer, but not just now when you are too occupied to read.

I will indeed pray a prayer for you both on Christmas morning in the Roman Catholic church at Kathgodam (or the River bed if the car gets stuck...)

My love and all good wishes,

R. K. Compton

Letter to Deepa from R. K. Compton

I almost did throw up that morning. Shaking like a leaf, with Miss Compton standing steady in the wings, I pulled up my stockings and approached the lectern. A last look, answered by a nod from Miss Compton, and I recited "Daffodils" from memory. I remember catching her eye again, just before the applause started.

The applause! Miss Compton hadn't told me about the applause. From then on, you couldn't get little Elizabeth off the stage! For every time I've metaphorically "pulled up my stockings" and pushed myself further out into the world (hundreds of times by now, including *Deepa's Secrets*), I owe thanks to Miss Compton, my goddess of gumption.

The food at All Saints was the opposite of inspirational. A lot of British food boiled beyond recognition, further drowned in "Indian" spices. The campus was set in the middle of some of India's best apple orchards. I may have eaten four apples, total, over the three years. We lived for the "sweeties" Mr. Fordham, the groundskeeper, stashed in his pockets, and "Smiley," the candy stand man who made Saturday afternoon visits.

I don't want to encourage your sweet tooth, but I'm also not going to get out Miss Compton's spanking stick and come after

All Saints boarding school

you if you indulge in a sweet. Let me suggest that at the end of a truly satisfying meal, we really won't have much of an appetite, not for food anyway. Often, we're just not ready to leave the table. Consciously staying at the table longer can help cut down on less conscious late night snacking in front of the TV or on your device.

While breakfast is arguably the most important meal of the day, our last meal of the day can impact our sleep. Overeating before bed will keep your body "up" digesting. And when we don't get enough sleep, our bodies produce less leptin (an appetite-suppressing hormone), which means we have more ghrelin (the appetite-stimulating hormone) running around in our systems. Our brains call for food (extra energy), and, not surprisingly, over the past few years, science shows a clear link between sleep deprivation and obesity.

There are certain foods that contain natural sleep aids— tryptophan in nuts, seeds, and bananas. There is melatonin, a natural sleep regulator, in tart cherries and grapes. I have created a handful of simple nibbles that fill the "dessert" bill—just enough sweetness without a heavy load of fat, or calories, in case you need an excuse to linger a little longer . . .

Mango Lassi

A lassi is the perfect summer refresher. In New Delhi, they were usually savory—yogurt-based with smashed cumin seed, fresh curry leaves, a little salt, served on the rocks. You can get a sweet lassi in India, but this recipe is a closer cousin to the American smoothie.

SERVES 4

4 cups fresh or canned mango pulp
2 cups Greek yogurt
1 teaspoon vanilla extract
2 teaspoon rose water
1 tablespoon wild honey
¼ teaspoon ground cardamom
¼ teaspoon salt

Mix all ingredients in the blender. (If you're using fresh mango and they are not sweet enough, add a little extra wild honey.) Enjoy!

Rose water *is made from the damask rose and it's been around since the time of Cleopatra. The distilled water steeped with petals is hydrating and cooling for the throat and the skin. Many, including myself, swear by rosewater as a wrinkle-preventative.*

Disappearing Leftovers: Double or triple your lassi recipe and serve as dessert. Pool the lassi on a plate, and top with berries and dark chocolate shavings.

Toot Sweet

Set a bowlful of Toot Sweet on the table after dinner. Not a single flavor is lost in this mix—intense chocolate, sweet, chewy fruit, salt, heat, and a hint of anise. All in one mouthful. A great snack or after dinner digestif. *Bus bus*—enough food!

1 cup dark chocolate nibs (Taza chocolate is a good brand)
1 tablespoon fennel seeds, toasted
½ cup unsweetened dried cherries
1 cup unsweetened dried cranberry
1 cup pistachios, shelled
⅛ teaspoon cayenne powder
⅛ teaspoon Himalayan or other fine grain salt

Put all the ingredients in a glass jar and shake to mix.

DEEPA'S SECRET
Chewing fennel seeds after a meal not only aids digestion, it eliminates bad breath. Ha!

"Focus."
—Susan Dryfoos

12

Comfort Foods

Scented Chai

Comfort Foods

Satiety is the opposite of anxiety.

urns out, Susan Dryfoos is a wonderful writer, artist, and Oscar-nominated documentary filmmaker, but I had already shared a fit of uncontrollable, mildly inappropriate laughter before I knew the first thing about her. We met in a dull boardroom back in 1996, although it feels more accurate to say we found each other—a couple of long-lost sisters, without the family baggage.

As we've each followed our artistic passions over the past thirty years, we've been the "why not?" to each other's "why," holding up the spiritual megaphone or the supersize flyswatter, whichever is warranted.

Five years ago, she hosted the most fabulous New York dinner party at her Upper East Side apartment. I can't remember a thing I ate, but I could go on about each of the other guests who shared that table. Really shared—Susan's professional success has to stem, in part, from this ability of hers to get people to open up. A prominent health journalist, a man of middle age, had been searching for professional relevance (wait until you're in that bracket), then cancer entered the ring. He was newly in remission, he told us delicately, and the mental reshuffling was practically audible around the table.

I jumped in and talked about my mad scientist kitchen-laboratory phase, our weight loss, and Thampy's new shot-free life, and I recounted the conversation with Dr. Baron at the second six-month check-up when I told him I was planning to send my results to *South Beach* Agatston. I do my Baron imitation, "Deepa, *you* should write that book!" The health journalist straightens up and interrupts, "Your doctor is right, you should." Next thing, the seven of them are talking about when, and how.

The following morning, Susan couldn't let it (or me) go. She held her hands up, as if she had her camera rolling, "Deepa, what is your earliest memory of food?" I start with *Mamma*, and when I finally slow down forty-five minutes later, Susan claps her hands. "Write it, write it all down, the way you just said it."

Susan Dryfoos at the Oscars

She must've called me back home in San Francisco another ten times with the same command. And I've breathed, "Focus," easily another thousand times to get to this point.

You can't get 14 chapters and seventy-plus recipes into a cookbook and diss the food—cooking and eating are very satisfying pleasures. But, there are times we try to fill up holes with food, hungers that we're then too stuffed to properly feed, hungers which food will never comfort.

Satiety is the opposite of anxiety.

I pressed myself to name a few of the emotional needs we all experience to some degree: the hunger for human connection, love, passion, purpose, adventure, or inspiration (a spiritual deadness) . . . for feeling whole, rest, restoration, downtime, freedom . . . for health, physical well-being, sex, certainty, movement or exercise . . . for harmony, peace in our world and the world at large.

Being fully present—conscious of everything everywhere at all times—is the general prescription. Fine, if you're a monk. I mean, I'm improving, but a hunger is often that little itch that keeps you from being fully anything. So, I challenged myself to come up with my own personal recipes, comfort "foods" that take care of these itches and again, I (with my spiritual megaphone) challenge you to make them your own.

No-Carb Comfort "Foods"

• Make something more beautiful—a plate, a table, your nightstand. • Light candles—in the bedroom window at dawn, at the dinner table, in the bath. • Linger—after a meal, in the car, in bed. • Sixty seconds or sixty minutes of gratitude—forget a journal, it's okay to be grateful for some of the same things over and over again. • Find nature—go a small or a great distance to find your place in the universe. • Really listen to music—yours and a best friend's. • Express yourself—I paint (oil portraits of people I love). Write, dance, build . . . • Arrange something—flowers, tools, drawers, a closet, a glove compartment. • Smell—spices, oils, flannel shirts. • Lean in . . . to the person next to you at the table, on the couch, in the bed. • Read offline. • Watch a sunset at home. • Make your bed, like you would for company. • Count your riches: family, friends, workmates, storekeepers . . . • Renew an old (when it's been more than a year) connection. • Give a knickknack away. • Plan a family vacation. • Grieve. • Remember the ten best smiles you ever earned. • Slip into bed early. • Walk everywhere. • Write a letter. • Look at old photographs. • Stretch from head to toe. • Take a bath, or a slow shower. • Steep yourself in a cup of tea.

Scented Chai

This last recipe is the perfect one to leave you with. Where I come from, friendships were made, renewed, deepened, and remembered over *chai*. Enjoy a warmed cup, new friend. So many pleasures, really. Plus, food.

SERVES 2

1 cup water
1 cup whole milk
1 tablespoon fresh ginger, grated
4 green cardamom pods
1 teaspoon honey
4 bags or servings of tea (Darjeeling or Assam black tea)

Bring the water and milk to a boil in a deep saucepan. As soon as it begins to bubble (careful it doesn't boil over!), remove from heat. Add remaining ingredients, cover, and steep for 4 minutes. Strain into a warmed teacup and enjoy!

DEEPA'S SECRET

Yogurt-honey face mask. Mix yogurt, honey, and ground orange peels (dried in the New Delhi sun!) and apply. Leave mask on for twenty minutes, then steam or wash off. I finish with a face rub mixture of equal amounts of rosewater and 100% vegetable glycerin (both available online). My skin never feels better.

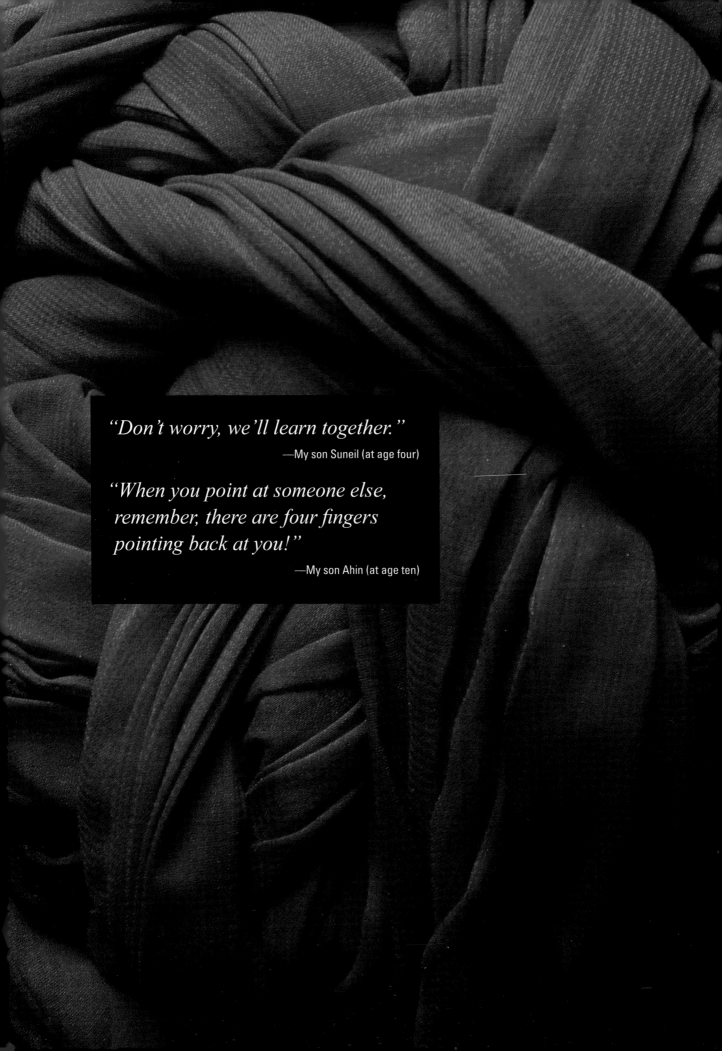

"Don't worry, we'll learn together."

—My son Suneil (at age four)

*"When you point at someone else,
remember, there are four fingers
pointing back at you!"*

—My son Ahin (at age ten)

13

Life in the Balance

Suneil and Ahin

Deepa and Ahin

Life in the Balance

"Indian food blooms at night."

—Suzy Becker

ife is a balancing act, or a juggling act, or both simultaneously, with a little dog act (whose trainer just quit) thrown in, and . . . it's showtime!

When our boys were young, Thampy and I each had our own ventures going. They referred to us as their high-tech dad and their low-tech mom. Most nights, we scraped ourselves together to make it to the table for family dinners. The meals were prepared with a premium on ease, not nutrition—it went in the win column as long as I got something on the plate and the same something didn't end up in the trash after the meal. (Please, that was way before composting.)

My sons have both been out of the house for more than twenty years now. I am in a sweet spot (let me say, with some nostalgia and hindsight, that they're all sweet spots)—between parenting and grandparenting.

I had both of my boys by the time I was the age they are now. I'll never forget confessing to Suneil, in calm exasperation, that I didn't have all the answers. I had never been a mom before.

No earnestness will ever match the expression on my four-year-old confessor's face: "Don't worry Mom, we'll learn it together."

It is not a small decision to pay attention to what you eat. It may, in fact, be one of the biggest, best decisions you make in your lifetime. And it's likely to throw off your balance in the beginning. Let's learn it together.

First, planning ahead—stocking your supplies (Chapter 4, p. 22) and planning your meals—actually saves time, and it also saves you from making squirrely, last-minute decisions. Give five weekdays a whirl with the menu planner below. You can shuffle the days around, and even the meals within the days, but make sure everything you need is in the house. None of my recipes should take more than an hour to prepare. And, most of my recipes can be made ahead and frozen or stored in the refrigerator. Indian food is said to "bloom"—its flavor improves—overnight.

You may need to scale down if you are cooking for one, or scale up if you are having company, or depending on leftovers. Try not to let your family-friendly dinners be dictated by your least adventurous eater. (Plenty of studies show that kids' food preferences remain fairly stable, and exposing them to varied, healthy meals is their best shot at a healthy diet in later life.) Kiddify the recipe: cherry-pick ingredients, flavor accordingly, and keep a reliable protein source (e.g., rotisserie chicken) on hand.

Eating out of the house provides a different set of challenges. It is easy to make your midday meals portable (it just takes containers), provided brown bagging is an option. When you know you're going to be eating out at a restaurant, it's worth previewing the

AT HOME/IN A HURRY	CASUAL COMPANY	SERIOUS COMPANY
Herbed Asparagus and Macadamia Soup (p. 98)	Herbed Asparagus and Macadamia Soup*	Herbed Asparagus and Macadamia Soup
	Dilled Masala Crab Cakes (p. 168)	Dilled Masala Crab Cakes
Green salad with Zingy Citrusy Salad Dressing (p. 39)	Green salad with Zingy Citrusy Salad Dressing	Green salad with Zingy Citrusy Salad Dressing
	Heritage Barley (Better than Rice) Pilaf (p. 66)	Heritage Barley (Better than Rice) Pilaf
		Mango Lassi (p. 194) with sliced mango
Chop Chop Lamb Chops (p. 182)	Chop Chop Lamb Chops	Chop Chop Lamb Chops
Heritage Barley (Better than Rice) Pilaf	Heritage Barley (Better than Rice) Pilaf	Heritage Barley (Better than Rice) Pilaf
	Sweet and Spicy Mango Salad (p. 114)	Sweet and Spicy Mango Salad
		Toot Sweet (p. 196)
		Kerala Fisherman's Prawns (p. 172) ** or Dilled Masala Crab Cakes
Ginger Cabbage Slaw (p. 122)	Ginger Cabbage Slaw	Ginger Cabbage Slaw
	Tousled Haricots Verts and Caramelized Carrots (p. 154)	Tousled Haricots Verts and Caramelized Carrots
Mughlai Sauce (p. 32), with store-bought rotisserie chicken	Mughlai Sauce, with store-bought rotisserie chicken	Mughlai Sauce, with store-bought rotisserie chicken
		Red, White, and Blue Berry Breakfast Salad (p. 86)

*served in teacups

** stick prawns on skewers to serve as an appetizer

menu. If nothing passes the test, don't give up! With the prevalence of allergens and special diets, most restaurants are very willing to accommodate your preferences; just ask.

Try these DIY restaurant "entrees"
- Roasted chicken
- Broiled fish
- Medley of vegetable sides
- Entrée-sized portions of salad
- A couple of appetizers

Ask for minimal oil and any sauces on the side.

It was my younger son, Ahin, who once said to me, "Mom, when you point at someone else, remember, there are four fingers pointing back at you!" (Actually, three in the correct version of the aphorism, origin unknown.) It's easy to let things—a restaurant or people; a partner or kids—stand in our way, even when we really want something. I can't make this work for you. But, I swear—all four fingers and a thumb on a stack of wholly healthy, entertainment-worthy recipes—*you can*.

"Don't look for approval. Approval comes on the day you are successful, and not one day before."

—Justice Anna Chandy

14

This Is Just the Beginning

Justice Anna Chandy

This Is Just the Beginning

My great aunt, Anna Chandy, was the first woman judge in all of Asia. As a kid, I had no idea what she did, but I knew she put in a long day. My uncle usually greeted us for dinner. His job as Chief of Police got him home just after five, most days.

My aunt would race in, kiss us hello, and head straight for the kitchen, her black robe flying out behind her. I wasn't an ardent feminist at the time, but I remember questioning the division of labor. "*Chittamma*, why?"

"Why do I make dinner for my family?" She clucked at me. "We choose our battles, Deepa *mol*." The meals were a measure of her devotion to the marriage. And there must have been war stories that recorded her rise to the bench, but they went with her to the grave. "If you want to do something, just do it," she admonished me. "Don't look for approval. Approval comes on the day you are successful, and not one day before."

The battle metaphor is dangerously popular—we battle weight; we battle cancer; we battle anxiety, traffic, and on and on. It's all well and good when we're winning, but what happens when the odds (biology, genes, ingrained behaviors, the environment) are stacked against us—does that make us losers?

Let's give up the "battle." There may be extra energy we bring to a battle, some psyching ourselves up to do battle, the mini-wins, and the pep rallies—but, it's exhausting. Food will always be the last one left standing.

Let's hold on to "choice." The first definition of "diet" in the dictionary is a neutral one: "the *selection* of food a person, animal, or community eats," not "restricts itself to, deprives themselves of, or eats sparingly." I'll repeat myself here: this is not that kind of a diet book.

It is a book full of choices, yummy-*swadisht* choices. No recording, calorie counting, "good" or "naughty" stickers.

You know yourself, better than anybody else does, anyway. You have some idea of your genes, your habits, your preferences, and your weaknesses. If there is a carb you can't do without, try eating less of it. If there is a time of the day you must eat, sit down and do it. Change over gradually, or all at once. As you begin to feel healthier, that feeling will become your new addiction. Feeling healthy (not hungry) is addictive. Trust me. That carb you couldn't do without—you may find a slow carb or no carb alternative. And, whichever numbers are important to you—pounds, blood sugar, afternoon productivity—they will move in the right direction.

Whatever works for you—that is what works. There it is, my secret: no cookies, no cookie-cutter approach. You got this book; now own it.

Wake either of my sons out of a sound sleep and they can complete this phrase: "Our mothers give us birth; it is up to us to . . . choose life." To the extent you have choices, choose wisely. Choose health, choose life.

I hope my food, your food, gives you great pleasure and good health, and that your healthy choices free you to find, do, be, and feel your best.

That's everything. Except the carbs.

"Bees do have a smell, you know, and if they don't they should, for their feet are dusted with spices from a million flowers."

—Ray Bradbury

"I want the cultures of all the lands to be blown about my house as freely as possible. But I refuse to be blown off my feet by any."

—Mahatma Gandhi

Acknowledgments

I'll start with my base: my husband (muse, and unofficial editor), Thampy; my sons, Suneil and Ahin; and their partners, Gabby and Jenn. I created these recipes for Thampy, I wrote them down to pass them on, and from there it grew. If you would just ask me once more, Ahin, "What do I need to do to get you to write this book?" I could so gratefully answer: "You did it, you all did it!"

Now, infuse that base with the essential contributions of Suzy Becker (my word-smithing magic maker and so much more), my miraculous book designer Craig Frazier and his gifted associate, Nancy Yee-Chan, my unstoppable agent Beth Davey, my tireless editor Kim Lim and her team at Skyhorse. And the belief in me, my way of cooking, and the *Deepa's Secrets* project, so enthusiastically expressed by FoodCorps' CEO Curt Ellis. Special thanks go to brand guru Jonathan Cranin, dear friends Vel and Steve Cox, my soul sister Susan Dryfoos, Gerine Ongkeko, and Jorge del Calvo. Valerie Crane Dorfman nourished me with kindness and lent me her English teapot for my *Chai* recipe photograph. To each member of the George family, I owe a separate debt—Ron (taster/editor), Barbara (platter curator!), Eric and Andrew (advisors), and Chris (for Beth!). Without you, this book would never have taken shape.

Next, layer on the expert food photography of Sherry Heck, who used natural light and genius to capture my New Indian cuisine with results that burst off the page. Fanny Pan's superb food styling and Zen-like patience was backed up by Kristene Loayza's meticulous knife skills, and the two share a wicked sense of humor, which made those marathon shoot days not just doable but also fun. I am also thankful for the work and friendship of the ever-buoyant photographer Marianne Nobre and the exquisite portrait of the Kerala fisherman and that ethereal sunset over the Arabian Sea, taken by our old friend, true renaissance man, Shyamal Roy. Special thanks to John Casado for sharing exquisite photographs from his recent trip to India.

I'd like to finish off by thanking my community of suppliers: well-stocked, farm fresh Bi-Rite grocery, Bryan's Grocery (where everyone knows your name), Polk Street's knowledgeable New India Bazaar, and Swan Oyster Depot (always the freshest). For photo props, I relied on super Courtney at SFSurfaces, Carol Hacker's Table Prop (happy hunting!), Hudson Grace, and Gumps. My family photos were patiently, digitally restored by Gabriel and the rest at Dickerman Prints. David Liu was a tech support savior along with Aaron Chang, and Ben Rosenthal is my nonjudgmental expert (not an oxymoron) Mac man. Thanks also to the gifted web designer Lucas Wager and Suzanne Baxter, who cheerfully provided graphic design assistance at all hours. Domingo Antonio Robledo's early recipe layouts were invaluable, and it was a joy to have the chance to work with Deepa Textiles designer Garima Dhawan again.

I would be remiss if I did not acknowledge Dr. Bobby Baron, and that first checkup which sent me back to my kitchen. Or Srijith Gopinath's (Campton Place's Michelin star chef) four-star appearance in my first video. The encouragement of Geeta Gopal and Williams Sonoma's Michelle Foss and Pat Connolly powered me through the project's early stages. My brilliant lawyer-niece Elizabeth Puthran has been generous with her time. And, my ingenious biotech friend Dr. Joan Fallon has been more than generous with her praise.

I may still be remiss—there are friends, too many to name here, to whom I feel a great sense of gratitude.

Forget pods and seeds and flakes—you have all been my life's "secret spice."

Index

About the Author

A graduate of Delhi University with degrees in journalism and political science, Deepa Thomas is the founding CEO of the internationally renowned Deepa Textiles. After twenty-one years and twenty-three awards, Deepa dissolved her ten-million-dollar enterprise to care for her aging parents. Four years later, a serendipitous conversation with University of California's Dr. Bobby Baron ended her self-imposed hiatus. Since 2010, Deepa has combined her passion for journalism with her newfound passion for cooking, deconstructing the principles of the most successful diets and healthy living practices in order to reconstruct a simple, slow carb New Indian cuisine. She has amassed hundreds of recipes, lost twenty pounds, and freed her husband from a ten-year dependence on insulin shots.

Deepa Thomas lives with her husband, not far from her two sons, in the Nob Hill section of San Francisco.

deepassecrets.com

Skyhorse Publishing books may be purchased in bulk at special discounts for sales promotion, corporate gifts, fund-raising, or educational purposes. Special editions can also be created to specifications. For details, contact the Special Sales Department, Skyhorse Publishing, 307 West 36th Street, 11th Floor, New York, NY 10018 or info@skyhorsepublishing.com.

Skyhorse® and Skyhorse Publishing® are registered trademarks of Skyhorse Publishing, Inc.®, a Delaware corporation.

Visit our website at www.skyhorsepublishing.com.

10 9 8 7 6 5 4 3

Library of Congress Cataloging-in-Publication Data is available on file.

Cover and book design by Craig Frazier
Cover photograph by Sherry Heck
Food photographs by Sherry Heck
Food styling by Fanny Pan
Page 160, 229 photographs by Marianna Nobre
Page 12, 48, 204, 210, 214 photographs by John Casado © Copyright 2017
Page II, 163 photographs by Shyamal Roy

Print ISBN: 978-1-5107-1898-2
Ebook ISBN: 978-1-5107-1899-9

Printed in China